AF255801

Simply Begin

Simply Begin

Create, Meditate & Find Purpose

Anna Marie Valentine

RESOURCE *Publications* · Eugene, Oregon

Contents

Dedication

As a little girl, I wanted to be a part of everything. I was a creative kid, and a pursuer of belonging and dreams. This book represents layers of my story that I could never have imagined as a young girl. This book represents the reality of a dream that I have always held of becoming an author and sharing my voice. This book is dedicated to every little girl with a voice, and with a dream.

I want to dedicate this book to my biggest hero, my mother, Mary Boyd. Thank you for always picking up the phone. Always finding a way to support me when I need you the most, and for teaching me the gift of selfless love. I have gotten to know Jesus through being your daughter, and for that, you have saved me.

I want to take a moment to thank my friends, Adam Stevens and Vicky Castain. These two individuals walked me through my years in graduate school, and always represented encouragement, fun, and creativity. Thank you for your friendship over the years, and for always cheering me on in new seasons of life.

Lastly, I want to thank my husband, Matthew Valentine. Your encouragement, collaboration, gentle spirit, and laughter has inspired me to venture on through the journey of Simply Beginning . . . What a joy it is to spend my life with you. I love you.

Introduction

"For this reason I remind you to fan into flame the gift of God, which is in you through the laying on of my hands. For the Spirit God gave us does not make us timid, but gives us power, love, and self-discipline. So do not be ashamed of the testimony about our Lord or of me his prisoner. Rather, join with me in suffering for the gospel, by the power of God. He has saved us and called us to a holy life—not because of anything we have done but because of his own purpose and grace. This grace was given us in Christ Jesus before the beginning of time, but it has now been revealed through the appearing of our Savior, Christ Jesus, who has destroyed death and has brought life and immortality to light through the gospel."

2 Timothy 1:6-10

The secret of getting ahead is getting started.

Mark Twain

Introduction/ What to Expect on This Journey

Allow me to set the stage. This journey begins with my hands on a keyboard anticipating the inspiration to begin typing. The blinking cursor of the document in front of me seems to be patiently waiting for the words to appear. I have a message to share, but the pressure of articulating it correctly makes the task a daunting one. This is the moment. With a sigh of relief, I find comfort in the fact that I already have a paragraph. This represents a struggle that I have experienced time and time again. After 31 years of life, you think it would become easier. I am referring to the seemingly impossible task of *getting started*, and taking another step towards the identity that the Lord has bestowed upon you. I have always wanted to become an author. But when it comes to specificity, I begrudgingly believed that the perfect idea would magically pop into my head. That had to be what it was like for JK Rowling right? Or C.S. Lewis? They had a moment of inspiration that cultivated in their legacy of words. But year after year passed, and I would become frustrated by the number of projects, books, poems, plays, and creative endeavors that were either barely started, or that were simply left as a "one day" on my to-do list of life goals.

As another year approaches, I did miraculously have one of those moments I longed for, yet it felt very different than I would have imagined. My curiosity, passion and creativity led me to believe that my bright idea would result in some magical fiction tale, or a Hollywood script. Yet what was revealed to me was the very topic that has seemingly stunted me throughout my life. Simply Beginning. As I sat here on my porch on January 1, 2023, I sunk into the wicker chair and gazed over the perfectly balanced pool in front of me. The computer screen in front of me consisted of a blank page. "This is the year I am going to write a book." I realized in that moment that my topic was within my struggle all along. My challenge was getting started and following through with each project. My challenge was trusting that the art that I so longed to create was already within my spirit. There is no amount of knowledge or wisdom that could take the place of my vulnerability here and now. Sure, in ten years (given I am given the opportunity), my mindset will surely look very different. But for today. I am 31. Today, I have been privileged to live a fulfilling, educational, and unique experience in this world. Today, it is likely that my struggles are shared with millions around the world. My experience matters. My *current* experience. Not who I was in the past, not who I will become tomorrow. It is the conflict within me that becomes relatable to the world around me. So, let's begin the exploration. Together. I imagine that this book will end very differently than it began. I imagine this exploration will delve into a journey of successes, frustrations, moments of rage, curiosity, growth, and healing. I will attempt to answer some big questions. I will fail. I will also succeed in the fact that I will not rest until I have answered these questions to the best of my ability given my 31 years of life. I ask for your compassion. I ask for your grace. And most importantly, I ask for your collaboration as we navigate this murky water together. My answers to these questions will surely differ from yours, as we all experience this world from a unique perspective. With that idea, it is important that you contribute to this open dialogue. For your experience may match up with other readers in significant ways. If you gain anything from the time that you dedicate to this book, I hope that it serves to create a journey of self-exploration, curiosity, and tools to help you take the next steps. I hope it places you on a new path. To move past your "stuckness" and embrace the wisdom that already lies within your spirit.

The most important aspect of my being is my personal relationship with Jesus Christ. Too often, throughout my life, I have white knuckled the idea that I can create meaning and purpose without first looking to Him. If you get anything out of this book, I want to remind you that the most important habit to cultivate would be to continue to explore your relationship with Jesus. In no way am I asserting that this will not take patience and hard work. In fact, the more that we surrender our lives to Jesus, the more clarity we will receive regarding his unique design for our lives. In John 5:17, Jesus says: "My Father is always at his work to this very day, and I too am working." A life of a Christian is not to cease efforts, pray and believe it will all work out. Rarely do I run across a Christian who says, "Once I became a Christian, life got easier." No, choosing to live a life with Jesus holds you accountable to renew your mind and body from the inside out, and that is hard work. In fact, I believe the life of a Christian calls us to surrender, pray, and then choose to act in a way that glorifies a Father that will strengthen us to the very end. A God that will inspire our hearts and meet us in our mourning. Whether or not you are a believer in Jesus Christ, I hope that my faith shines through the pages of this book and displays how He is working in my heart and mind.

Chapter 1: The Blank Page

I want to begin this book with a story. I don't know about your experience, but stories are the main vehicle by which I feel able to understand the world on a deeper level. Whether it is through performance art, my conversations with patients and friends, or a good novel—story telling us what allows us to share the commonalities of our humanness. Stories are relatable. Stories can be gut wrenching, heartbreaking, or inspirational. Sometimes stories can encompass all of these things at the same time. Stories depict emotions which are daily human experiences that send data to our brains about what is happening around us. We can talk about emotions all day long, but stories allow witnesses to feel similar emotions co currently. Stories are limitless.

I want you to think about a time when you started something completely new. For myself, I want to use the example of my yoga practice. When you make a conscious choice to begin something for the first time, emotions begin to activate. For me, I starkly remember showing up to a class for the first time and feeling drawn in by the peaceful atmosphere. The smells were soothing, and the studio was small, yet inviting. This studio was tucked behind Washington Square Park, right on Bleeker Street. I was attending graduate school at New York University, and Greenwich Village was my stomping grounds. As I rolled out my mat, I remembered immediately thinking about the state of my underworked body. I did quite a bit of walking and had a long history of dance and some weightlifting, but this environment was starkly different. As we began the flow, a million different thoughts began to race through my mind. "What was I thinking? Everyone here definitely knows how confused I am. This hurts. How is this relaxing? When will this be over?" The battlefield of my mind immediately navigated to comparison, insecurity, and embarrassment. At the time, I had no idea that harnessing the mind was a foundational element of yoga. I remember toughing out the class because it felt like it would be even more embarrassing to walk out. At the end of the class, the instructor guided us into savasana, also known as "corpse pose". If you have never taken a yoga class, most classes end with this pose where you are positioned on your back with your palms shining up towards the ceiling. In that one moment, all the self-deprecating thoughts began to cease.

Making the decision to walk into a new season of life always comes with complexities. While change and evolution are constant, entering a new season often comes with components of loss, excitement, and uncertainty. I would like you to think about a time when you moved away from what you considered "home". Maybe you were leaving your home at the age of 18, or maybe you were planting new roots in search of your next home. No matter which example you choose, your new rhythm of life is emerging, and the beginning stages are hard to interpret what the new season may end up looking like. Your former creature comforts like the coffee shops that you often pursue, and a good friend living down the street are no longer within your tool kit. Knowing where your grocery stores are located, and taking the route to your local gym are no longer possible without the help of Google Maps. Over time, we typically adapt to the environment in which we have found ourselves in any given season of life. New patterns of life begin to take root, and we often grieve seasons of life that seem simpler. Sometimes we regret not practicing more gratitude for the simple rhythms that kept us grounded because we were so focused on the next steps. I want to refer to this process as a "season of seed sowing", which requires patience, discipline, faith, and action. This is a season that will require your attention time and time again as you evolve into different seasons of life. This is a process that always looks different but essentially follows the same pattern. If we can start to become familiar with how this process generally looks, we can better formulate how to walk through it with successful, meaningful results.

My fingers explore the keyboard. I am waiting for my brain to respond to the challenge placed directly in front of me. Doubt is seeping into my brain space as I anticipate how this experience could easily mirror past experiences of abandonment. There is a well-known concept that most art is left in a graveyard because it was not realized. While this is morbid, it can be important to consider.

Reflecting on this idea, I have a choice. While I could dwell in all the unfulfilled experiences that I have abandoned, I must also take space and time to note the goals and achievements that I have sought through to the end of their seasons. A few that come to mind immediately include my master's degree, my journey working at The Menninger Clinic, a few bodybuilding competitions, a plethora of musical theater performances, and dare I say- my acceptance of my yoga journey as a *practice rather than a destination*. Why do these memories evoke such a sense of accomplishment? The answer is easy. Each of these experiences have a distinct beginning, middle and end. What is more satisfying than seeing a goal lived out from the beginning to the end? That is the same expectation that I believe colored past experiences with creative endeavors. And I must confront the weakness that contributed to the decision to stop prioritizing or believing in my message. I commit to this project to be quite different in that discipline will fuel the process. Whether or not there are days where this feels far from my desire, or my inspiration is lacking, I will attempt to commit to giving this book my best effort. The rationale is clear. If I can work through the challenge during the setback, this will create hope that you can also walk out the same process. I am sure you are wondering why on Earth I feel so passionate about this concept, and I would like to share a bit of my heart with you. I realize, understand, and accept that I have a small perspective of everything this world has to offer, and the experiences that human beings are faced with in different socioeconomic statuses, in different areas of the world, and with diverse backgrounds. I see the world from the lens of my personal experience, whereas you see the world from yours. I believe that this is IMPERATIVE to promote compassion and understanding. If we can hear each other's stories, and relate to certain emotions and experiences, we can generate more grace and love for our fellow man. To help articulate this concept, let us look to:

> Matthew 22:37-39: Jesus replied: "'Love the Lord your God with all your heart and with all your soul and with all your mind.' This is the first and greatest commandment. And the second is like it: 'Love your neighbor as yourself.

Jesus gives us simple instructions to help guide the life of a Christian. If we are continually breathing in the wisdom of His good and perfect word, we can get to know who Jesus was, and begin to love others as Christ loved. I believe that a huge misconception of being a Christian is to "choose to love everyone and not judge". There is truth in this statement. It is not our job to judge, but it is our job to stand up for our hearts and our faith. 1 John 4:18 asserts:

> "There is no fear in love. But perfect love drives out fear because fear has to do with punishment. The one who fears is not made perfect in love."

Love does not mean we play the role of the pushover, fake, nice Christian. Love means that we hold our loved ones accountable for their actions, and we ask for the same in return. Love from a Christian is bold. Love from a Christian is not self-seeking. Love from a Christian is pure. This is how our Father instructs us to be in relationship with others, and this is also how we are to be in relationship with Him. Bold love is not meant to trigger shame, although it is possible. Bold love is meant to help us align with the compass that God has placed within our souls. If we can continually come back to this compass, He will guide our stories. Like yoga practice, we can always come back to the child's pose while in flow. We have the autonomy and authority to choose at our own pace. And to be frank, the pace does not really matter if we are continually coming back to the Father.

The purpose of this book is to help you position yourself to move forward into life with purpose and intention. This book is not just about sharing a myriad of stories. This book begins much earlier before that process. This book speaks to *simply beginning* to share your story, idea, or creative expression by attacking the blank page in front of you. Sure, you have a choice. You can choose to abandon the blank page. Allow shame and culture to tell you that your story is not important, or that your suffering has no meaning. Or you can allow your narrative to impact the world. I am here to declare that not only is your story important, but it is also a crucial component to combat the evil of this world. You must understand that everything you have gone through up to this point is valid, painful, and not okay. A deeper truth is that at some point, we have all played the role of the villain. Surely in the lives of others, but most importantly, in our own. I can assure you (without even meeting you) that you have likely been harder on yourself than anyone in this world. In fact, I would imagine that you have done your fair share of beating yourself up mentally. And we are not designed to live in the shame of our fragmented parts. Yes, there are real consequences for our actions. Yes, we must take accountability. And yes, your actions did represent your health and choices. Taking a hard look in the mirror can feel impossible for some. And while this process is deeply painful, it can also be incredibly liberating, and kick start your own healing process. I believe that we all experience a diverse range of emotions, regardless of the color of our outward appearance, or the status of our socioeconomic situations. Of course, some populations can experience emotions more intensely than others, and that would be a whole new book. I do want to highlight the emotion of shame. Shame equates to the concept that "we are bad people, or something is inherently wrong with us". Shame is a common emotion, and can be felt in smaller doses, but often shame can become all-consuming due to its assertive ability to have us question our senses of self. As a counselor, I often help individuals to identify their emotion of shame and walk them through rejecting that shame rather than drowning within it. Hebrews 12:2 says:

> "And let us run with perseverance the race marked out for us, fixing our eyes on Jesus, the pioneer and perfecter of faith. For the joy set before him he endured the cross, scorning its shame, and sat down at the right hand of the throne of God."

Again, we have another example of the life of Christ. He despised the shame. If we can identify the feeling of shame in our own lives, we can question its legitimacy, and surrender it at the feet of Jesus.

When we begin to transform shame, we go through our own personal heart surgery. We begin to take a closer look at our personal habits and patterns that are feeding into the shame, and we start to consider ways to live life differently. Shame can be a result of things that have happened to us, and/or how we chose to respond to what life through our way. Again, here we are not simply falling into victimhood, but also taking responsibility for our role in the story. I do want you to believe that there is a possibility of *transforming personal pains into your purpose*. Transforming that suffering into an opportunity for healing and sharing. If we choose to heal simply for the selfish desire of peace and contentment, we are doing our fellow man a disservice. The apostle Paul wrote a letter to the church of Philippi to encourage them to see past their circumstances and lay their lives and gain solely at the feet of Jesus. Paul himself was in prison when he shared the following message. Philippians 1:12 states:

> "Now I want you to know, brothers and sisters, that what has happened to me has actually served to advance the gospel."

Could it be that your story has been written as a testament to serve the gospel? I am not blatantly stating that your pain is justified, but I am asserting that regardless of your pain, our healing can only come from what Paul articulates. Our mission is to lay our life humbly at His feet and allow Him to work through our stories.

I want to point out that it is not always your darkest trauma that creates opportunity for creativity. Take this book for example. Without sharing any of my personal traumas, I have shared my dilemma with you. I am unable to commit to writing a book for fear of "not knowing how to begin" or "not believing in my ideas enough to round them out". Together, we are exploring this conundrum, and it has also inspired this book. The lack of direction has created a full lump within my chest. There it is. Doubt creeping in again to convince me that this endeavor will end just like my previous attempts. But I am here to tell you that I believe this experience will be different. Just by typing these words, I feel like I have been able to gain control of my mindset and shift the trajectory of this book.

Now I want you to try. What is something you have attempted time and time again that tends to end with the same result? Maybe it is relationships? Maybe it is keeping a fitness regime? Maybe it is holding consistent employment? Or broken friendships? Here is my invitation to stop assuming your future will be more of the same suffering you have experienced historically. The power lies within your ability to acknowledge the patterns. If we can become aware of the patterns that get in the way of a different result, we immediately hold immense power. I am referring to the power to *rewrite your narrative.* In my work as a psychotherapist, this is the crux of my job. We analyze an individual's lived experiences to determine what behavioral or psychological patterns are keeping them feeling stuck. Feeling trapped in the way that things are. Once we identify the pattern, we can open new lanes for the brain to process the world differently. We can explore new behavioral patterns for the person to implement consistently into their life to result in a different reality. What I am saying is that we have the power to determine our own reality. I am not simply saying, if I believe that I will be affluent and at peace, it will happen. But I am saying that regardless of my circumstances, I have the power to make meaningful changes in my thinking, and in my life. For one purpose. To humbly lie our pain at the feet of Jesus and commit to a life of service and obedience. It is not natural for human beings to surrender to obedience. We have a selfish belief that we can figure out life on our own terms. In my work with hundreds of patients and clients, I cannot deny the same reality that I have witnessed time and time again.

> *When we white knuckle our way through life, without a mission to heal and serve, we become lost, rigid, bitter, and angry.*

I understand that this is a generalization, but I urge you to ask yourself if you have noticed this in your own story. I am asking you to take a true deep dive into your spirit. If you can relate in some way to the statement above, I encourage you to continue reading.

There is one theme that I encourage you to keep in mind as you journey through this book. The story of our lives will cause us to stumble and fall as well as pick ourselves back up. This is a cycle that will continue to play out as we enter new seasons. I want to remind you of a gift that is always accessible to you. Remember that you have the power to actively choose to remain hopeful and optimistic. Life without hope and the promise of tomorrow will inevitably lead you down a road of fixation on the storms in our lives. Understand that peace comes after the storm has passed. Hebrews 10:23 states: "Let us hold unswervingly to the hope we profess, for he who promised is faithful." So, hold onto the hope of this process, and remember to choose optimism.

I can only imagine what you might be thinking. Sure, Anna, let's use self-affirmation and only look on the bright side. That is not at all how I want to tackle this subject. My hope is that you gain the skill of increasing your optimism, no matter the circumstances. Again, if your pain is meant to advance the gospel, the floodgates of opportunity begin to pour out. Later in this book, we are going to take a hard look at human suffering. I share this to express that human life will always be accompanied by challenges, both circumstantially and emotionally. There is power in accepting this truth. If we are aware that storms will come, we can better understand the best ways to navigate them. Again, the apostle Paul offers ideas in the book of Romans regarding how to live a "holy" lifestyle". Romans 15:13 states:

> "May the God of hope fill you with all joy and peace as you trust in him, so that you may overflow with hope by the power of the Holy Spirit."

I pray that the hands holding this book will begin to recognize that you are meant for great works. Your broken past does not mark you as unworthy. In fact, your past is what makes you the perfect person for the mission ahead. Stop criticizing yourself. Stop holding back because you are "unhealed". Start to walk out in faith. Remember that you are holy. You are anointed, and you are IMPORTANT. It is time to get started.

Reflective Pause in My Process: I have reached the end of January 2023. I have been working on this book for one month. The way that this book has taken form is a mirror representation of my thought life. It feels scattered and messy. It is a wealth of too many ideas, and not enough structure. It was directed and organized at first, and now it seems to be a treacherous unknown hike that leads me into the uncertainty of how it will end up. To practice what I preach, I am using the process as an opportunity to welcome all the confusion, knowing that a habit in the past would have been to turn back and come back from where I came from before I started. But again, where does that get me? Following my pattern of creating yet another unfinished project. So sure, some structural changes may need to be established as I continue my path forward, but I am choosing to address the process rather than turn away. Remember, using the word "yet" can help with increased optimism. For example: "I have not figured out how to express my objectives in this book." Let's switch that to "I have not figured out how to express my objectives in this book . . . yet . . . " See the shift in perspective!

Chapter 2: Taking the First Step

The first time that you engage in anything new evokes all the demons of uncertainty. How often does a middle schooler walk into the building on the first day of sixth grade with no anticipation of what is to come? There is a reason that many of us choose to find contentment in how far we have come and choose to stay still. *There is comfort in what we know, and fear in what we do not.* If we never go on a first date, there is no risk of heartbreak, right? If I never go to college and pursue that degree, I can never fail my class or disappoint my parents, and I will not have any student debt. I can understand this logic, and there is NO harm in contentment. That is the goal. But when we make excuses for allowing fear to get in the way of our larger purpose, this is lost art. In no way am I assuming that everyone should take chances and risks. No, it is simply not that straight forward. So many different layers come into play when an individual decides to make an important life decision. If you are familiar with the world of psychotherapy, you might have heard of DBT or Dialectical Behavioral Therapy[1]. In this modality, there is a concept known as "the wise mind". Essentially, this idea posits that individuals tend to make decisions based on logic and reasoning mind or with their emotional mind. Wise mind states that there is a gray area in between that is the sweet spot for aiding in discernment. If you have ever heard the

1. See Recommended Reading

phrase "Think with your head, not your heart", I am here to convince you to embrace the murky space in between.

Now let's address one of the biggest hijackers of creativity. It is a sneaky little voice called "doubt". As a follower and believer in the Holy Spirit of Jesus Christ and his teachings, I believe this to be the greatest enemy working his way into your life to offset your purpose and plan. On Tuesday evenings, I "seva" at a local yoga studio. If you are unfamiliar with this term, seva refers to "an act of compassion above oneself". And I will not lie to you either. I am compensated for this work by means of cost-free unlimited classes, which is not the true nature of the service, but it certainly is a gift I accept with respect. Additionally, the classes benefit my mind and body in a way that helps to keep me aligned with my spirit of service above myself, which also aligns with the teachings of Jesus Christ. Romans 12:1 state:

> "Therefore, I urge you, brothers and sisters, in view of God's mercy, to offer your bodies as a living sacrifice, holy and pleasing to God—this is your true and proper worship."

Galatians 5:13 states:

> "You, my brothers and sisters, were called to be free. But do not use your freedom to indulge the flesh; rather, serve one another humbly in love."

Philippians 2:3-5 states:

> "Do nothing out of selfish ambition or vain conceit. Rather, in humility value others above yourselves, not looking to your own interests but each of you to the interests of the others. In your relationships with one another, have the same mindset as Christ Jesus."

Lastly in Mark 10:42-25, Jesus taught the act of service to his disciples. He asserted:

> "Jesus called them together and said, "You know that those who are regarded as rulers of the Gentiles lord it over them, and their high officials exercise authority over

them. Not so with you. Instead, whoever wants to become great among you must be your servant, and whoever wants to be first must be slave of all. For even the Son of Man did not come to be served, but to serve, and to give his life as a ransom for many."

When you begin anything, an overarching theme with creativity is to create something new in and/or for the world. Generally, we are inspired to use our own gifts and talents to create, co-create, collaborate, or reinvent something as an act of service. I'm sure Taylor Swift doesn't put her heart on display for purely selfish reasons. No, she uses her own unique experiences to use her gift of music to share art with the world. So maybe you are in this boat asking, "okay Anna, I hear you, but what can I create?" While I appreciate this question, I cannot answer it for you. No, true creativity and vessel for sharing can only come from your heart. Take a moment and ask yourself what kind of art or activity have you been inspired by in the past? Maybe you are driven by politics or Ted talks. Maybe you are a creative mover or dancer. Maybe you enjoy scrapbooking, blogging or photography. Heck, maybe you just like dogs. I am not asking you to dig into your inner prodigy. I am asking you to note what inspired you or has inspired you throughout your life.

With that in mind, I also want to recognize that we change, transform, and evolve our identities over time. While I may have been inspired by punk music in my teen years, the range of diversity in my music has certainly expanded. This example illuminates the importance of welcoming new forms of yourself. Change is uncomfortable, and if we can master the art of welcoming change, rather than allowing it to keep us the same, creativity can take form in your life. *The past may inspire, but the present is where we want to start this journey.* The past can inspire or teach, and the present is the only true reality of who you are. Here and Now.

Have you ever clung so hard to a past version of yourself that you struggle to embrace who you are in the present? I know that I have made this error. For instance, maybe you have fond memories of your years playing soccer, and you look down upon your current state because you believe these were your glory years. This is a common pattern that I see clients get stuck in as well as myself. *If we resist change and evolution, this often leads to apathy.* Take for instance the example of becoming a parent. If a mother is so connected to her earlier years as a free-spirited world traveler, the transition into becoming a mom could potentially lead to despair as she begins to wrestle with the fact that her life will never look the same. She may ruminate on the grief that this chapter is in her past. Clinging onto the past is dangerous territory. So, I invite you to step forward with confidence. The future will never look like the past. This is a fact. Sure, we do not fully abandon things that made us who we are today. Sometimes we do choose to move in a completely new direction. It looks different for every person. A wise mentor once told me, "How we greet transition lies the foundation for what the next chapter of our lives will be". I believe this to be true. So let us honor our pasts, no matter how bright or dark, and move forward with the confidence in who we are and who we are becoming. We were not designed to stay the same. 1 Corinthians 14:20 states:

> "Brothers and sisters, stop thinking like children. In regard to evil be infants, but in your thinking be adults."

I believe that we were strategically designed by a creator. We were designed to mature. This begs another question. What does maturity mean? From a psychosocial perspective, maturity is the ability to respond to a given situation "appropriately". Erik Erickson was a German American psychologist and psychoanalyst. He developed a theory for the structure of development and divided his stages up by age spectrums. When thinking about Most of my readers may find themselves in the 10-40 age stage of Erickson's developmental theory. He calls this stage "intimacy vs. isolation". Essentially, Erickson found generalized conflicts that continue to present themselves in different stages of our lives. How we choose to overcome these conflicts determines the quality of our experience and overall mental health. Intimacy vs. isolation speaks to a person's ability to develop healthy connections and relationships, or to allow shame to keep us isolated and lonely. I use this to shed light on the importance of community and relationships in your life. I am not necessarily speaking of romantic relationships, although this is an element of this stage. I am speaking about the quality of the relationships that you have in your life, and how that may be an important factor of your "stuckness".

So how do we take the first step? What I am about to share is both logic and emotional. I would like you to start by making a commitment to yourself. Although you may not even fully understand what you are committing to, *write down* your personal commitment statement below. Examples will be provided:

Example Personal Commitment Statements:

- I commit to follow through with taking classes in photography and dedicating time to my craft weekly.

- I commit to showing up more authentically in my friendships and cultivating time to create a community where I live.

- I commit to taking time to explore new places regularly and prioritizing my desire of expanding my worldview.

- I commit to starting a website for the entrepreneurial project in the next three months.

- I commit to finding a space to serve, engage, and get to know other people.

____

____

____

____

____

____

For the next step, identify what key themes are holding you back from simply beginning. This book will refer to these identifiable barriers as your "Sabotage Dialogues". A few lines will be provided, but this is something that is an integral piece of showing up for yourself. If we are unable to hold a mirror to our own patterns, it will be impossible to change behavior. Again, a few example statements will be provided.

Examples of Sabotage Dialogues:

- Starting this feels too overwhelming, I wouldn't even know where to begin.

- Financially, I need to focus on work and my family.

- I do not have enough experience to do what I wish I could.

- I have tried before, and I always end up confused and lost and disheartened.

- Putting myself out there is just not me.

____

____

____

____

____

Reflective Pause:

Every day I write, I recognize my own sabotage dialogues. The more I recognize them, the more I feel as if I am starting to outsmart my own thoughts. The same doubts that have led me to losing traction in the past seem to be forging the fire moving forward.

The mindset has sincerely shifted from "I do not know what I am doing" to "I am doing this- this uncertainty is my process. This uncertainty is living." For me, it has promoted so much hope and excitement for what is to come rather than "this will never happen" or "this will only be successful when . . ." With that, I want to shift into the next chapter of this book, and of this process. Amazingly enough, it also has not been a straightforward timeline of writing. Often, days have gone past when I have not picked up my project, yet I keep coming back. Sure, life gets in the way, but I always remember my personal commitment to myself: I commit to writing a book. I do not care how it happens, but I will write a book this year. I have a message to share, and if I can impact one soul through this journey, my duty has been done.

The next method to the implantation of beginning is to establish "systems". A commonly overwhelming area for creativity is the limitless opportunity to move in any direction. If you have any level of anxiety like most of the population, this can be a perfect window into overthinking, causing unnecessary stress. I am suggesting that you start with an organization of your thoughts and expectations for yourself. This gives you a rough map into the exploration of your goals and ideas. Let's begin with the organization of your thoughts. This could be something simple like a brainstorm dump. I often find iPhone notes full of reminders, quotes and factoids that I do not want to forget. Maybe this is where you start. Whatever method you choose, I highly recommend getting your thoughts out onto paper. In a way, that is what is happening for me now as I articulate my thoughts. Secondly, let's discuss personal expectations. As we addressed earlier in this chapter, understanding personal commitments is a key factor in this process. Let us direct our minds to the expectations and deadlines that you might document. If we have set goals and deadlines, we tend to feel much more accountable and responsible to follow through. Just as a friendly reminder, this book is focused on the act of simply beginning. With that said, ambiguous planning can help the process to feel supported even when we do not know which direction we are headed.

So, it's time to devise a plan. Right now. Even if the anticipated goal is fluid in nature. Break your process down into manageable steps and place date deadlines in your calendar. I cannot emphasize timelines enough. We all need some accountability with planning and projects, and this is a very simple way to get started. While the process may take a different form as your story changes, we want to start with a strong foundation. One method that tends to feel more digestible is quarterly goals. Let's take my authorship of this book for example. If I were to commit to writing a book, that may feel like a finalized task, but when I break this down, there are so many additional moving prices that accompany this process. Hiring a literary editor, creating book query letters, researching publishers, researching publishing methods, reading other books . . . ect. My first quarterly goals may read something like the following:

- Continue daily writing to the best of your ability.

- Finish an overview of what to expect in book.

- Research methods of publishing.

So, as you can see, my quarterly goals do not read "writing a book", rather I have broken this process down into a few steps that allow me to feel like I have some control when the reality is that control is an illusion. Sure, there are consistencies that we can develop to attempt to create structure out of uncertainty, but we must also learn to accept flexibility. If you think about your life like an ocean, there are never ending seasons of weather. There will always be days when the water is calm. These days are important to sink into, appreciate, and engage in restoration. As humans, we also recognize that incoming waves could arise at any moment. This uncertainty tends to develop into anxiety and anticipation of "what to expect". The truth is, we can never truly prepare for what we do not know. I would argue that even if we DO know what is coming, preparation will often not stop the waves from crashing. If the country has been aware of what was coming with the pandemic that began in 2020, I would assume that we would not have entered that season calmly. No, I believe that the true anticipation of what was to come would have created chaos throughout the world. When we were met with certain decisions and truths, there was still chaos, and we engaged in resiliency, connection through disconnection, and horrific outcomes that may or may not have been prevented. I share this example to depict the nature of human experience. We are engaging in the creation of history right now. How many times do you look back on certain seasons of life and think, "If only I could go back in time and appreciate (fill in the blank . . .)."

Take a moment to consider your current season. What does the weather of your life depict in the here and now. What are certain things that you may look back upon in the future and think . . . " I am glad that I was as present as possible during that time" rather than "I wish I could have gotten my head out of the clouds". This concept goes back to intentional optimism. Again, not to invalidate the current storms you are experiencing. In fact, many of those storms are most likely excruciatingly painful. But where are some of the smallest consistencies that are keeping you going day to day. You are reading this book, so to me, that is an example that you recognize and consider your mental health, and you are taking steps to evolve into the next chapter of life.

Maybe the steps seem small, but I can assure you that they are integral, and worth recognizing. Writing this sentence is .005 percent of the process of getting this book published and into the hands of my readers, but without this sentence, this book may never become a reality, taking the shelf of thousands of wasted ideas that have kept their value hidden within the depths of my insecurities. I beg of you, take the next step, no matter how small. The world needs your gifts. We live in a country full of unrealized dreams and ideas. How can we continue to A.) Understand one another & B.) Learn from one another if we allow fear and shame to silence our greatest tool, our story. Because of our cultural and human desire to fit in and not be ostracized or disconnected from society. To me, there are no more excuses. I am not saying this will come easy, I am telling you that YOU have been called. Dig down into the depths of your unique person, and ask yourself, what is it that I need to create? Ambiguity is the beginning of honing your craft, but by asking the right questions, you will see that your purpose evolves through searching. If we were to create a sculpture out of a block of marble, the first carvings would not show us much, but the more we can dedicate to this project, the shape comes to our awareness. So, what are you waiting for? You now have the right questions; you have some prospective ideas of organization and implementation. And most importantly, you have your unique experiences, story, and mind. The only thing stopping you from searching would be your lack of respect for your story, or the lack of healing from your story. If we are afraid to look back, we do not have the encyclopedia of our lives to reference. I encourage you to seek the support of a professional if you feel there are areas that are too dark or scary to walk towards in your mind. Not just for the purposes of creating your purpose, more for the purpose of generating your healing. I am sure you have heard the phrase "Hurt people hurt people", so to me, therapy is not purely selfish. Your life will impact those with whom you interact, and if we can maintain the health of our own minds, we can have positive impacts on those around us. But when we continue to live life unhealed and controlled by our suffering, our relationships also tend to suffer. Imagine an angry person in traffic yelling obscenities? This would be a perfect example of someone using their pain to inflict pain. Though if that person was more centered, they would be able to engage in more acceptable distress tolerance. I obviously do not want to invalidate mental illness. There are chemical imbalances that impede individuals' ability to cope with the world around them. I understand this, but I also understand that the longer these individuals go untreated, the longer they will inflict pain on our culture. There are also moments when we might "snap". Our plate is overloaded, and our capacity is full. Our brilliant mind and bodies give us signals to remind us of our capacity. Honor your body. Slow down and take a breath. When you are ready, imagine what you would "like to be doing" vs. what you "must do today". I invite you to take one step towards a goal or dream. The time is now. What are you waiting for?

Chapter 3: Overcoming "When the Time is Right"

Well, for starters, the only time that we have for certain is now. While this may sound morbid, there is no security in the next five years, let alone the next five minutes. Pricilla Shrier is a powerful woman, mom and preacher who really struck a chord with me in one of her sermons. She emphasized how "if you are 30, but you only live until 40, you are pretty old" or "if you are 50, but will live until 100, you are pretty young". Time and age are both constructs of human existence to have some kind of measure to predict where we are and who we are in time and space.

When I was 16 years old, I went to the movies at a luxury shopping mall in Dallas, TX to celebrate a girlfriend's birthday. My mother was waiting at the mall to pick me up after the movie ended. I remember texting her that the movie had ended, and that we were going to grab some gelato on the way out of the theater. My friends and I split ways and I recall calling her cell phone several times to try and figure out where she was waiting for me. With no response, I walked out of the theater to find that my world had been utterly shattered in the duration of two minutes. My mother's car was parked sideways in the valet line, and I immediately knew that something was very wrong. As I approached the side of her truck, I observed the side windows had been shattered. As fear consumed my mind and body, I ran around the side of the car to witness that my mother had been shot in her face. Her dogs were shuffling as blood covered the truck and my mother appeared lifeless. As crazy as this sounds, I remember screaming, rushing to grab the dogs, and thinking "I cannot get blood on this new shirt that she bought me." Isn't it crazy what runs through our minds amid pure terror? I had little sense of what was running through my brain and impacting my physiology as the next few hours turned into a chaotic blur. I remember riding in the ambulance with my mother in the back. I remember a kind woman offering to take our dogs and left me with her phone number. I remember every soul from my high school flooding the emergency room, while all I wanted was to be left alone. I remember a kind woman who allowed me to stay in her home that night. I remember how big her shower was, and how overwhelmed I was to have such an array of shampoos to choose from using. I remember the blood washing away from my hands, face, and arms. I remember not understanding whether my mother was alive. That is all I remember. The man who shot my mother that night was a man of color who had a history of assault with a deadly weapon. Everything that I understood about the world in which I lived was about to become so much more confusing. Because of the luxury of the shopping mall in which this happened, our family, home and story were plastered on the news for weeks. While my experience was a tragedy, our story got excessive attention for several reasons. We were an upper middle class white family, and the population around NorthPark Mall was affluent, white, and terrified. We also began receiving hate mail describing how we did not deserve the attention we were receiving, and how oppressed communities would never get this sort of attention. While this is true, it felt as if the opinions of our circumstances forgot that we were human. Certainly, this attention and space of power benefited us and white privilege in this case and did not help the larger issues of racial injustice at hand. In fact, that is a deeper darkness, and this event was a result of those deep wounds. I can understand that, and I will always do my part in educating myself further and acting with the intention of anti-racism. And this was still my mother. The attention on our family after this event was nothing short of harassment. I recently watched the documentary "Harry and Meghan". While we were not members of the royal family, we certainly got a taste of ruthless, compassionless, abusive media.

I share this story for many reasons. Selfishly, this book gives me the opportunity to share my story from my perspective, not some skewed version from the media. Secondly, the point of this chapter is not to induce fear, but it is meant to remind you of how uncertainty is the only certain part of life. Greek philosopher, Heraclitus asserted the notion that the only constant in life is change. I venture to take this a step further and say that the only constant of life is change and walking towards uncertainty.

I am not sure how I can better articulate how important it is to create in the here and now. With no idea of how much time you have, your voice is what encourages new perspectives and change. My own healing process has taken on many forms. I have taken deep dives into educating myself on how and why events like my mother's take place. I have processed this event over and over in therapy, and a catalyst to my healing journey was actually, believe it or not, a creative endeavor. During my years at New York University, I was offered the chance to take part in the writing and creation of a piece of therapeutic theater. The title of the script was going to be: "Behind the Doors: Terror in the Home and World". With a story like the one I have shared, I assumed that I might have a perspective to integrate into this play. I wrote a monologue, which I will insert below. When it came to the rehearsal process, I concluded that I must bow out to keep my healing process safe. The rehearsals became overwhelming, and I understood that I was not yet ready to openly share my story. The director asked if they could still perform my monologue, and I agreed. When I witnessed the performance at The Providence Playhouse in Washington Square Park, I reached the pinnacle of my own healing. Another actor performed my piece with so much grace, respect, and power. As I sat in the cold, audience of the dark theater, I was offered the space to hear my story performed, with no direct connection to who I was, and I was able to experience catharsis, tears, and a deep understanding that we can serve one another in these ways through theater. Although your creation may not take the form that you envision, maybe that is the purpose. That is the process.

I Don't Wanna Go There from: *Behind the Doors: Terror in the Home and in the World* [1]

Nope, I don't wanna go there.

But I am there a lot. In my mind. In my sleep.

For 8 years now.

Sometimes, I wake up in a panic trying to wipe the blood off of my arms. Ever heard of a pseudo seizure?

When my mind wanders . . . Remembers.

My stomach feels sick. Sweaty palms.

I can feel my heart pound through my chest.

I don't know if I am anxious or nauseous.

Too much adrenaline.

White shorts.

I don't want a hug.

Purple shirt.

I don't want a casserole.

White slip on vans.

I don't want your thoughts.

Gold earrings.

I don't want kind words.

Drenched in a sticky red tye dye.

I don't want prayers.

Just get it off of me.

The concrete is speckled with the red liquid as well. Like splatter paint.

I don't need a ride.

Or an extension on my paper.

1. First performed in *As Performance* Therapeutic Theater series at NYU Program in Drama Therapy.

I don't want your false sympathy.
I don't understand this longing to have a connection with someone who is experiencing what it must feel like in hell. Stay away.
I want to be paid no mind.
Like I was before.
I don't wanna go there.
I went there.
I spoke of what happened.
I feel angry a lot.
I have a lot of rage.
I kicked through a laundry hamper and broke it just this morning.
I have a lot of guilt.
I don't want to be singled out.
Or treated differently.
Because this happened to me.
But that is hard to avoid.
But then again,
It didn't happen to me..
Or did it?
Witnessing violence is overlooked.
Because what does it really mean?
I witness violence everyday at my internship.
And sometimes, I wish it was me that would get hit.
Instead of someone else.
Seems so senseless.
Something about that idea seems right.
Being the witness.
Seems unimportant.
"Be glad it didn't happen to you."
But I helplessly watch it happen to other people.
And then . . . what happens to me?

Reflective Pause:

Well, I told you I was going to be honest with my process of beginning, and here is what I have experienced this far. I can't stop. Now that I feel like I have some direction, it is just flowing. No fancy inventive new research. Just my heart. In all its layers. My experience of the world. Think what could happen to you if you were to simply get started by exploring your heart. Not a revolutionary idea or reinvention of the wheel. Just your true heart. Written out on paper. What are you waiting for?

A popular term in American Culture is this idea of boundaries, which as a therapist, I certainly believe are important to address. I also believe that in the hustle and bustle of our lives, this important concept can become skewed and misinterpreted. You see as our lives change and evolve, so does our capacity for what we allow. Our time, heart and mind are our most valuable resources. It is our responsibility to discern how to use these tools. The ways that you are sharing are most likely personal and noble feats, but if they come with the cost of our families, does this align with what you value most? In the next chapter, we will explore your personal values, and normalize how they shift and evolve as life transitions. You see, the more we expand our role repertoire, the more life begins to take different shapes. If we can adjust to shape shifting, we can assume more peace in our lives as the wind blows. For example, in college, I was a part of a show choir, a full-time theater student, a friend to many, and I worked at a tanning salon. My life was full of fun as I got a taste of the world outside my parents' home. I was very privileged to have parents who supported me in my endeavors, and therefore, I had plenty of time and energy to play and find out what I liked and didn't like. As life evolved, and I entered graduate school, it was a rude awakening when I started to realize that I could not juggle play and graduate school. My priorities were shifting, my roles were shifting, and I wanted so desperately to cling onto the routines that I was familiar with in college. Looking back, I could have saved a lot of searching by accepting my shape shifting with optimism and acknowledging the grief of change. As I entered the workforce, I was a single woman living in New York City. I dedicated all my time to work, training, physical fitness, and again, traveling the country. When I made a big move to Houston, TX, I had the opportunity to work at one of the top mental health hospitals in the country. For me, big changes had begun to happen consistently and regularly. While I would like to think I adapted well, I think that my resistance to letting go was one of my biggest hurdles. In Houston, I found space for play and ended up working on a few musicals to supplement my work life. This is certainly not something I regret, but the magic did not feel the same as it did in college. For one, I was surrounded by beautiful people from all walks of life, but I struggled to relate to them as my life was in a completely different season. I kept busy, and through my business, I continued to refuse to accept the shape shifting. I bought a house during the 2020 pandemic with the intention of finally settling into my life in Houston and slowing down, except I did the exact opposite. I met my husband just two weeks after closing on my house. At the time, I had no idea, but life would offer me a platter of choices that almost became too much for me to bear. After dating for two years, my husband and I were left with options. He was moving to Florida to continue his medical training. Knowing this was the man I wanted to spend my life with, there were two choices. We could pursue long distance, or we could go ahead and start our lives together. When my husband proposed to me, I knew in my heart what choice I would make. What I didn't know was that I was about to face a season of grieving and celebration that were going to dually co-exist. I resisted the idea of becoming a wife out of a desire to keep life the same, and a deep fear that I was "too damaged" to measure up to the woman he deserved. Another change was beyond my comprehension. And not only one change, but God would lead me through a season of loss to aid me in facing my biggest fears. Fears that I had stored away for years. With engagements, I have often heard "you will learn who your friends truly are". This always confused me because this was a conventional time to celebrate, right? After I was engaged to my husband, I lost a handful of friends who had become my community for the past two years. While I believe this was spiritual warfare, it never made sense to me as to what transpired. Juggling friends and a serious relationship did prove to be very challenging for me to navigate. I prayed, spoke to my therapist about this, and did my best to practice discernment. But the loss of these friends was just the beginning of a season of suffering emotionally, physically, and mentally. Now when I reflect on this time, I know that I was experiencing grief, but I was unable to recognize it, so no WONDER it was so confusing to process. With our move to Florida, I sacrificed a job that I loved as well as selling the home that I had lovingly settled into. While these were hard decisions to make, there was not one moment I questioned whether or not this was God's plan for my life. This light kept me aligned, as well as immense love from my husband, family, and dear friends. I knew that to continue shape shifting, I needed to welcome the change, and let go of the rest. Easier said than done right?

Now please do not get the wrong idea. I am not saying that abandoning a life that you love to follow your heart is the answer. In fact, I do not believe in one truth path, but I do believe in following the Holy Spirit as you feel moved. When my friends became distant, I found myself night after night alone in an empty three-bedroom home. I took frequent walks and spent 6 months on my knees asking the Lord to help me walk through whatever was going on within my spirit and heart. The most helpful action I took was to reach out for spiritual mentorship. The pastor who married my husband and I was always a call away. Dave was a family friend who had been in my life for 10+ years. I remember telling him that I was afraid I was "losing myself". I will never forget the words he said to me. He said, "Anna, wherever you go, you will always be Anna". That was a lightbulb moment for me. I knew God was calling me to make these transitions, but I also knew that God would not would never trick me. God would never try to change the core of who I was, I was always there, and He was always there alongside my journey. As my wedding day approached, a peace started to fill my soul that I had never experienced before. The turmoil of trying to make "the right decision" started to fade.

I was stuck in a world between what culture depicts and what the Father was placing on my heart. Culture said to "do you and forget everyone else". My heart said, "follow me, Anna. Trust me Anna." And I stand here today, writing a book, which is something that I have always dreamed of doing. So again, my storm may seem strange to you, and my storms will not look like yours, but what I have learned is that we can only gain the life we are meant for by following our heart, mind, and spirit. Culture emphasizes logic, our hearts purely emphasize emotion. The key is to take them all into consideration and invite the spirit to help you decipher your path. In Dialectical Behavioral therapy, the blend of rational mind and emotional mind is referred to as "wise mind."[2] I also want to add another layer which is our spirit. If we can merge all of these, we can discern how to walk-through transition and change, as well as how to honor grief as it surfaces. This is wisdom that I simply was unable to identify as I walked through it. Now I feel more prepared than ever to face change, grief, and uncertainty with a heightened awareness. All the emotions can and will co-exist, and it is up to us to respond accordingly, and to embrace gratitude and optimism about the future chapters of our lives.

Let's reflect on the question at hand. How will we know when it is time to make a change? The truth is that we are changing with each breath. Change will always happen around us, but it becomes our personal responsibility to actively pursue change in our own lives. I believe this change starts at a heart level. Analyzing the state of our heart is arguably the most important step when assessing where we find ourselves in our own story, and what we foresee as possibilities for the rest of the book, that is our lives.

If you imagine your heart as frozen, it can feel impossible to feel the warmth of an optimistic tomorrow. As we mature and develop into the unique identities of who we choose to become, we cannot avoid the suffering and heartache of living in a sinful, painful reality. If we meditate too often about this, we start to develop ice crystals on a childlike heart that was once warm and hopeful about the future. I certainly want to acknowledge another painful

2. See Recommended Reading

reality that many individuals do not land in a picture-perfect representation of a pure, idealistic childhood. No, most individuals must learn to cope or adapt to the darkness that they witness. Where there is darkness, there is also light.

John 1:5 states:

> "The light shines in the darkness, and the darkness has
> not overcome it."

If the word of God as the only truth, we can have great hope that with the trials, there is always hope. I am going to challenge you to honor your own resilience by recognizing that there can be no light without the darkness. Your personal darkness is the key to your freedom and to your change. Do not hide the darkness. Use it as a springboard into the light.

> "The night is nearly over; the day is almost here. So let
> us put aside the deeds of darkness and put on the armor
> of light."

If you are a movie buff like me, this section has reminded me of "The Dark Knight Rising" where Christian Bale is captured and thrown into the "The Pit", which is an ancient, underground prison at the bottom of a dark well. Please skip the following paragraphs if you do not want to spoil the movie for yourself. The prisoners can only see a sliver of light at the top of the well which represents their untouchable freedom, as only one other prisoner in history was known to have escaped. Christian Bale's character, Bruce Wayne, knows that escaping this prison is what holds the only possible future of his home city of Gotham. With his calling leading him, Bruce takes the leap and can successfully escape the captivating. I understand that we are certainly not all Batman, and I also understand that trials are going to be different for each unique human story. In fact, Stephen Spielberg was denied entry into USC's film school three times before his career began. Sylvester Stallone lived in a bus station and sold his dog just to get $25 to live off shortly before writing "Rocky". I do believe that the only "right time" to do anything will be determined by your own discernment and the state of your heart at any given time. We may make decisions that have consequences that we did not anticipate, and if we are walking with the Lord, I do believe that He will guide our steps. Every step of the way. Through the suffering. Through the celebration. Through the darkness, and into the light.

Chapter 4: But Where Do I Begin?

I want to start this chapter by sharing some thoughts on where NOT to begin. I want you to read this meditation and then spend a few moments with your eyes closed reflecting on what I am about to share with you. The chefs' recommendations include a distraction-free environment, ideally outdoors. Instrumental music is highly encouraged.

For the purposes of this exercise, I would like you to reflect on all your daily responsibilities. Feel free to include work, relationships, school, daily activities of functioning (laundry, bills, cleaning, cooking, exercising . . . etc.). Additionally add in things like volunteering, religious commitments, how much time you spend on television, surfing social media, crafting, socializing. I want you to account for everything. Organizations you are a part of, friends that you support through different functions. I want you to visualize it all on a portioned plate of your life. Now I would like you to assess whether your plate is appropriately full or if it is overflowing with Thanksgiving leftovers. What responsibilities are you committing to your life, your energy, your attention, and your spirit towards right now in this season of life? Take a pause here and reflect for a few minutes. Set a timer for 3-5 minutes and examine where your spirit is being utilized.

Now this next step may not seem so easy, and I want you to meet the resistance that may come along with your response to this idea. I would like you to consider what you can shed from your plate. In her book "Overwhelmed" Brigid Schulte makes a remarkable reflection on how the art of being so busy is now trademarked as a badge of honor in American culture. Sure, your endeavors may be genuine. Maybe you are a member of many organizations in which you desire to have influence. Maybe your social circle is like that of a college fraternity. Maybe you volunteer at every school event of your child's life. These are certainly noble feats. These are important, but it is time for you to recognize your window of capacity and tolerance. Human beings have a limit to how much time and energy they can submit to different domains of their life. I want you to really meditate on how you are spending your time and energy. Are they aligned with what is most important to you? Are they motivated by the exhausting rhythm of trying to change your image? Are they actions to manipulate how others see you or how they view your character? I know these are difficult questions to answer, and I understand. I have asked these questions of myself regularly, and I am often disappointed with my honest answers. But I am also here to tell you that your past does not define your present. There is a quote by Erik Erickson that states: "We do not go to therapy to change the past. We go to change the future." I have always appreciated that quote because it helps to redirect our minds towards what lies ahead, and how we can learn from our past to inform how we want our future to look. We can all become disoriented as we try to navigate the complexities of life, but that is also the beauty. Without the process of life, we might live like stagnant robots. Thankfully, we have this beautiful gift of emotions, that allow us to find meaning and purpose, but also expose us to pain and suffering. Though I also believe we cannot experience one without the other.

Reflective Pause:

This process started like a dart train. I was so clear about my vision, about what I wanted to create. Six days have gone by, and I feel like the flame is dimming. As with other projects, this is an opportunity. I have the option to abandon this work, to prioritize other tasks of my life, or I can continue to press forward. My commitment at the beginning was to see this process through to the end. I am not sure if any of you have ever experienced this dimness, but I can acknowledge that this is a space that feels familiar to me. So, with that, I acknowledge this, and I choose to press forward. Anxiety and doubt may say "Good luck, or do you really know what your vision looks like?" And to be honest, of course not. I do not know what treasures this book may uncover, but I believe that this dip is an important part of this process and journey. Here's to pressing onward and believing in the power of creativity.

Creativity amazes me because it does not have a structure. As a type A individual, I love clear direction. I like to understand what my goals are specifically, and what steps I need to take to fulfill them. With creativity, one must embrace the process rather than the product. And while the pages of this book will will come to a hault, that does not mean the ideas generated come to a halt. In fact, my vision is very much the opposite. I want this text to provide you with a springboard into your ideas and dreams. If we can apply some of the concepts that I am boldly expressing, maybe it is time to begin a new journey for yourself and your unique voice.

So back to the question at hand, where do you begin? Well, the fact of the matter is that you have already begun. By simply continuing to read this book, that signifies to me that you are interested in revealing ideas that are already within your spirit, or you are one of my first readers and you are doing me a favor by editing my work. To those individuals, thank you and I love and appreciate your generosity of time. For the readers who are interested in exploring their own creative potential, I want to commend you for taking the time to consider some of the ideas I have offered. I want to pause the book to allow space for a creative activity. The idea is to give you a foundation to work from on your own journey. Grab a hot tea or cold beverage of choice, some pen and paper and allow yourself to engage in the writing process below.

1. Take this space to highlight the domains of your life. Maybe this includes different roles that you identify (Ex: Caretaker, worker, advocate), and scale the level of value or importance

you place on this area on a scale of 1-10 (1 being of least importance, and 10 being the highest level of importance). I will supply an example below:

Daughter and family member (9), Therapist (7), Wife (10), Spiritual Person (10), Cook (4), Adventurer (7), Fitness Enthusiast (6.5), Student (6), Artist/Creator (4)

2. Now I would like to explore whether your daily life and activities align with what roles you feel are the most important to you. For example, if my highest rated role of spiritual person is a 10, am I taking time each day to dedicate my time, spirit, and energy to this domain?

3. Finally, I want you to highlight the roles or challenges that you feel are getting in the way of aligning your priorities with the life that you desire.

(For example, mine may be "shameful person", or "insecure person", or even "anxious and avoidant person").

The last step is critical because it allows us space to consider our tough realities. These roles are not excuses, rather they are characteristics within us that we must come face to face within order to better understand. By developing our relationship with ourselves in its truest form, we can get a clearer understanding of where we desire to devote more energy and time.

So now that you have a clearer grasp of how you are showing up in this present chapter of your life, this gives us traction to be able to make distinct headway towards our goals, dreams, and ideas. I also want to articulate the notion that these roles, priorities and values change as life evolves. For example, in college, I was heavily dedicated to my role as a musical theater performer. While this was a noble feat, my life circumstances have evolved. There will always be an artist and performer within me that inspires my future trajectory, but my priorities are shifting, and that is okay.

Now let's transition. I can imagine this book has got your mind buzzing with your thoughts and ideas, and I would like to take a few moments to emphasize the imperative practice of quieting the noise. I once had a professor in my PhD program share the following concept: We have a body, but we are not our body. We have a mind, but we are not our mind. Simply, we are pure consciousness. As someone who finds meaning in introspection and creativity, this took me many months to consider what this meant. I share this to also show you that this process I underwent was the very opposite of what my teacher was positing. Here I was, trying to overthink and process what he meant, rather than surrender to the possibility of this distinct truth. As human beings, we long to hold on to our identity and what we know. Whereas, if we can take a step back and recognize the truth of this statement, we can begin to master the ongoing feat of taming our minds. So why is this important? If we are unable to find stillness in this moment, and in every moment, our minds tend to take us on a wild goose chase of thoughts. So yes, it is imperative to harness our ideas to live life to them, but if we try to operate this machine through the lens of past experiences, cultural influences, and untethered notions of "how we should be or do," we will lose consciousness along the way. The biggest anchoring force of our identity surely comes from the Lord Himself.

Exodus 14:14 commands us to be still:

> "The LORD will fight for you; you need only to be still."

You see, we think we must figure it out all on our own, when truthfully, our stories are already laid out for us by the design of the Lord. We can choose time and time again to try and forge our own path, or we can choose to listen to the spirit which dwells within each one of us.

Our culture is starting to pick up on the benefits of daily meditation. And I can imagine what you might be thinking right now. Yes, Anna, we are aware of this, and it doesn't work for me. I want to offer you an alternative route to embracing more meditation in your everyday life. You see, meditation refers to mental discipline. The purpose is *not* to relax you or clear your mind. The purpose is to train your mind like a warrior in the same way an athlete may train for a game or competition. The same professor that I referred to earlier in this text referred to this process as "becoming martial artists of our own minds". And while you may be thinking, "Absolutely, yes! Let's do this", here is the reality. This practice is entirely possible, the act of training our minds to automatically wire to responses of maintaining peace in our relationships and souls, and it is a lifelong practice. You see, there will always be waves in the ocean that take us off guard or continue to thrash our little boat around. The human stress response is designed to respond to threat, but we must differentiate what signifies threat and what is *self-perceived* threat. For example, say you are working as a clerk at a grocery store, and you have a customer who is unregulated and upset that their coupons are not working. While unfortunate, this is not a threat to your life (in most cases). Rather than internalizing this as stress, is it possible to see this as an opportunity to respond with patience and grace. Who knows what else this woman has going on in her world that these coupons are impacting her so significantly. I also do not want to accept this behavior as "okay". It is not appropriate. But how we respond directly impacts our level of peace. Her emotions, and the ripple effect of those close by who are watching this interaction. This process is possible by becoming aware of how the stress of daily life impacts your brain and body. Awareness comes with a higher level of accountability. I often think of the ability to self-regulate from a developmental perspective. We cannot hold a baby to the same standard that we may expect of you, the individual reading this book. Awareness is one of our most important tools, and it comes with a level of responsibility. We cannot change what we are unaware of in the first place. So, what does this all mean for you, my reader. My hope and desire are that you will use meditation as a way of embracing life as it comes.

James 1:19 asserts to:

> "My dear brothers and sisters, take note of this: Everyone should be quick to listen, slow to speak and slow to become angry."

Practically speaking, this represents the posture of a meditator who allows their practice to lead the way in which they respond or choose not to respond to the world around them.

Reflective Pause:

Once again, here we are to check in. As I sit in this office, I am feeling a bit lost in this venture. My ideas are flowing, but not in the way I imagined. When I first began, this project made complete sense to me; however, as I continue to press forward, this book feels as if I am trying to follow directions, but keep making unassuming stops at the gas station, or taking turns that are not in the original directions. Rather than allowing my brain to turn around, I choose to continue to follow whatever path this leads me towards with the hope that it will all come full circle. All of this information is important and is obviously a part of this process. Rather than considering this book as a finished product, I want to venture in whatever way my heart and brain are leading me. I have certain skills and knowledge for a reason, and I choose to continue the journey, rather than to let another spirit inspired project melt through the cracks of self-doubt and frustration. Rather, I choose to embrace the confusion and frustration. These are the emotions that will allow this art to become real, relatable, and important. See you on the other side of the journey.

Chapter 5: The Purpose Lies in Your Suffering

I would like you to think about a few of your favorite movies or books. Most good stories do not simply contain details of a seamless life with moments of gratitude and joy for the simple moments in life. Most good stories become powerful because they contain a certain level of human suffering. Let us consider "The Hero's Journey" again. We begin with a protagonist or identified "hero". The hero goes on a journey. Amid this journey, the hero is put to a series of tests by which the character attempts to navigate through, which is a blend of successes and failures. Towards the end of the story, the character usually winds up with new insights and philosophies into the meaning of their suffering that they can approach with action. So, you see, if we are always searching for a way through life to wrap up like a present with a perfect bow, we are not accepting the reality that life demands resilience through suffering. If we avoid difficult tasks, we can become anxious energies that shame ourselves for not facing adversity, or we try to make excuses to support our avoidance, and yet something doesn't feel right about the course of our path. I once was posed with a quote, "The only way out is through", and the more that I age, the more this seems to be the only path to righteousness.

1 Corinthians 1:30 states:

> "It is because of him that you are in Christ Jesus, who has become for us wisdom from God—that is, our righteousness, holiness, and redemption."

To ask you to embrace the suffering is a task that I would not wish upon my worst enemy, but I will ask you to welcome the suffering. We can choose to ignore the suffering in this life, or we can invite it in for a warm dinner to get to know its relevance. One of my personal favorite pieces of literature is a poem written by Rumi entitled "Your Body is a Guest House". Rumi was one of the most acknowledged Persian poets who is one of the most popular poets in America. The poem uses the metaphor of a house to describe how emotions come to our front door. The poem goes on to emphasize the concept that we have the opportunity and responsibility to welcome our emotions like house guests. Without choosing favorites, or ignoring emotions we dislike, we can learn a great deal from each one of them.

Your Body is a Guest House[1]

Listen, oh beautiful soul.
Every day a new feast
comes running into your life.
Always a new experience.

Your body is like a guest house,
receiving company from the hidden world.
Some are positive,
some are tragic,
and still others who are frantic.

All mirroring your needs.
All showing you ways to expand.
All challenging your beliefs.

Whoever that comes from these unseen lands,
receive it without regret.
Welcome all that come to you,
with no judgment.

1. Rumi, *Beloved*, 13.

Remember, every visitor,
here a short time,
meant only for your growth.

So, while it can feel invalidating to simply say, "be grateful for your suffering", a huge cognitive shift is available when you start to notice the gifts from your suffering—whether that is gaining personal resilience, wisdom, or experience that helps you relate to others in their suffering.

I am an individual who loves to read about the history of authors, actors, artists, and even my medical doctors. I will do research to learn a little bit about who they are and why they do what they do in this world. I am usually always comforted to read about how their personal stories influenced their professional career. For instance, reading that a neurodivergent public speaker found his work by growing up in a culture where he felt dismissed. Or that my nutritionist found the beauty of holistic food through a diagnosis of her own eating disorder. For me, this helps me to trust what I input and who I ask for help. For me personally, the vulnerability of reading about how suffering paved the path for their future has allowed me to cognitively shift how I respond to personal suffering. I am certainly not devaluing the pain now. Whatever your suffering is, sometimes it is prolonged or does not have an end in sight. I often consider grief. For those who have gone through loss, I am sure you can relate to the idea that grief does not go away, yet our relationship to it shifts, evolves, and changes over time.

Take a moment and consider the concept of "purpose". What does this mean to you? For me, it represents acting with the intention of making the world brighter. Purpose looks different and unique to every human being on this planet. For some, purpose evolves from taking care of others. For others, the purpose of serving their political beliefs is to advocate for their values. Some individuals find purpose in simple, everyday tasks. I am asking you to dig into your perceptions about your own purpose. What does it feel like to embrace your purpose, knowing this is an ever-evolving state of being. For example, I feel fulfilled in my purpose when I have moments of discovery in the realm of therapeutic relationships with my clients, and I also feel purpose when I make a homemade meal for my family. It does not have to be a black and white answer. If you are curious in carving out a better definition for yourself, I would ask that you identify your personal values. Values are your own personal morals, ethics, and help to decipher your way of behaving and interacting with the world. Values can serve as a personal compass to help us understand the "why" behind our actions and decisions. Maybe your values are rooted in a foundation of honesty, integrity, family, and financial security. Possibly your values include things like advocacy, personal growth, education, or spirituality. To help guide your path, here is a word bank to pick and choose from. This is just scratching the surface, so feel free to add in your own values, change or personalize the linguistics to fit your personal experience:

List of Values

- Honesty
- Integrity
- Travel
- Career
- Hope
- Discovery
- Mindfulness
- Independence
- Financial Security
- Wisdom
- Family
- Freedom
- Spirituality
- Modesty
- Peace
- Responsibility
- Community
- Creativity
- Support
- Simplicity
- Humor
- Commitment
- Gratitude
- Nature
- Joy
- Parenting
- Order
- Harmony
- Adventure
- Advocacy
- Uniqueness
- Kindness
- Connection

Now let's explore a lesser-known exercise. The following ***anti-values*** are common human patterns that tend to show up in our dynamic experiences. If we allow them to fill too much space, they grow like weeds, overpowering our personal desires and actions. I feel like these are important to highlight because they can give us a clearer picture of what is taking root in our experiences, and how we are responding. There are many reasons as to why we can allow these seeds to multiply, but if we are able to recognize how prevalent these "anti-values" are in our own experiences, we are beginning the long process of uprooting them. The first step is acknowledgment and awareness. Below you will find another list. This list is not meant to induce shame, rather it is to equip you with more recognition of what might be holding you back from taking the step towards where you ultimately want to end up. This list is not exhaustive, but I do encourage you to pick 1-3 "anti-values" that might be running your everyday life. Once we have this data, we can start to really get to the crux of what rooted these ideas in the first place, and how to practically decrease them over time.

Anti-Values

- Anger
- Anxiety
- Chaos
- Comparison
- Conflict
- Control
- Doubt
- Drama
- Divorce
- Disconnection
- Fear
- Insecurity
- Isolation
- Reactiveness
- Self-Consciousness
- Self-Loathing
- Shame
- Victimization
- Worry
- Substance Use

By now, we should have developed a clearer understanding of who we are, both in our strengths and in our personal battles. I want to take a moment to commend you for making it this far. First, you are choosing to spend your precious time reading a book because you trust that maybe there might be some useful information or guidance. Secondly, you are bold enough to take a reflective look in the mirror.

Now I do not believe that a simple list of values and anti-values can help you truly understand and identify your personal purpose. In fact, I also believe that purpose is an ever-changing spirit that evolves as we grow and mature. I do believe that this culmination of reflection could help you in identifying your personal battles. Now why is this important, you may ask? This is not only important, but also an integral part of your hero's journey. Individuals do not relate to the poised final picture. No, individuals tend to relate to the suffering, and find hope through observing others who have persevered through that suffering. If we ignore the demons within our story, we either remain in denial or victimhood, neither of which leads to personal growth and/ or resilience. Power lies in naming your demons, acknowledging their power, and using your strengths to find new life and restoration. Take for instance, Romans 6:4:

> "We were therefore buried with him through baptism into death in order that, just as Christ was raised from the dead through the glory of the Father, we too may live a new life."

As a therapist, I have observed individuals who will do anything in the world to avoid taking a long, hard look in the mirror-myself included. I have also observed the power of addressing this reflection as a steppingstone to their personal liberation. Another beautiful truth is that this is not a journey that you must navigate on your own. I may be biased, but I would argue that attempting to take this path solo will only lead you into confusion. We may feel alone in our struggles, but the truth is that every human reaches a place where reflection and introspection is a necessary component of maturity and growth. I am not suggesting that everyone have a counselor, but I do highly recommend it. Wise counsel is like "honey to the bones".

Proverbs 15:22 states:

> "Plans fail for lack of counsel, but with many advisers they succeed."

Wise counsel can be such an invaluable tool. Not only does it help to provide you with clarity in your struggles, but the power of human connection is also present. Proverbs 27:18 states:

> "The one who guards a fig tree will eat its fruit, and whoever protects their master will be honored."

This is also not a journey that has to take place in a short period of time. This is a unique, personal journey that may take years to better understand. That said, we can start to recognize the vices or distractions that we use to avoid this journey. Once we can eliminate the safety precautions we develop to avoid, we automatically place ourselves in a healthier space to listen, reflect, receive, and transform. I will add one last list to this chapter that may serve to help you acknowledge the vices or distractions that could be preventing you from growth and liberation. I certainly believe that things like technology and work have a place in our lives, but when we start to depend too much on external comforts, we take the risk of impeding our relationship with ourselves. Look at the list below. I am in no way demonizing the items on this list, but I am asking you to see what stands out to you.

Vices/Distractions:

- Technology
- Social Media
- Netflix/Streaming Services
- Co-dependent relationships
- Power
- Work
- Food (Restriction or influx)
- Spending Money
- Dating
- Status
- Fame
- Gossip
- Substances
- Negativity
- Victimization

Reflective Pause:

As I continue to pave this path forward, I feel as if I am navigating into an unknown rainforest. I am inspired and pulled in different directions, yet I do want to stay on course towards our shared goal. There are many different paths that we can take to get to this goal, and the next season of writing will take me down many crooked paths. Some of these paths will make the final edit, and others will have to find a new home. I choose to honor whatever comes and keep my rough draft to reflect on this journey of the birth of this book. While you are here for different reasons other than following my personal journey of writing a book, I feel as if sharing this process could help you to normalize the complexities of forging forward your creative, unique path. We are human together.

Chapter 6: Purpose Lies in Welcoming Your Suffering

This chapter is meant to generate something many people are afraid of welcoming. We will tread carefully through the nuances that embody a person's response to trauma. You may be wondering what I am referring to. I am identifying the formidable ability to experience hope. Hope can be a tricky thing because we risk disappointment, we set ourselves up for potential rejection, and most importantly, we walk the tightrope of change. I would argue that the fear of change is the key to most creative's "stuckness".

Change requires us to make, create, and do something differently. Change asks us to take risks. Change can ask us to put ourselves out for the world to see, or even put our hearts on the front lines of human mockery. Change requires us to expand our perspectives, our minds, and our possibilities. Change asks us to walk a new path, whereas comfort tends to whisper, "You can trust me, you know me." How often do you let comfort take the place of potential change or creativity? Granted, I understand that there are many layers to this notion. We can make every excuse in the book for our stuckness, and the truth? Your excuses are valid. We live in a ruthless world where we are never immune to suffering. There may be seasons of your life in which the suffering takes place in your home, and there will most definitely be suffering in the culture around you. We can choose to ignore suffering and pretend as if it does not pertain to us, or we can begin a process of befriending this experience and understand its purpose to make sense of our purpose.

Romans 8:20-22 states:

> "For the creation was subjected to frustration, not by its own choice, but by the will of the one who subjected it, in hope that the creation itself will be liberated from its bondage to decay and brought into the freedom and glory of the children of God. We know that the whole creation has been groaning as in the pains of childbirth right up to the present time."

As hard as we try, we cannot escape the suffering of this world. We cannot protect our children from understanding this for themselves as they mature. The only thing we can do is equip ourselves, and our families to sustain through the storms. This is another book, but I do want to refer you to Ephesians 6- The Armor of God. This chapter is invaluable and offers the proper tools to have in place as we prepare to conquer suffering in our life.

I want to offer you a weapon to help you navigate the suffering, rather than wading in the gloomy waters of grief. What if it is possible to acknowledge the suffering as a doorway to new life, rather than staying in the pit of despair? I am not telling you not to grieve. In fact, I encourage you to acknowledge every emotion you can identify as you experience the deepest pitfalls in life. When we fail to acknowledge or express the emotional signals our brains are offering, they can fester within the very cells of our bodies. Emotional identification is a critical step to welcoming suffering, and all that it brings. Suffering is a term that blankets a never-ending list of experiences. Suffering to a child may be the loss of their first dog, while suffering to an adult might be a family member receiving a terminal diagnosis. The mission here is not to invalidate the pain of the suffering, rather to formulate ways to move through whatever season you find yourself within at any given time in your life. How we choose to interact with our experiences often sets the stage for what the next season will bring.

So, you might be wondering how this plays out. "Okay Anna, I can acknowledge the suffering in my life. In what way can I possibly use tragedy?" Every story is different and unique in its own ways. Some individuals use creativity as a vessel to their healing, while others cannot even begin to explore until they are at a certain point in their grieving process. If you know my background, you may know that I spent 10+ years studying and making theatre and art. Immediately, I think about the tragedies and comedies of Shakespeare. Shakespeare's first folio of writings are often remembered as intense dramas and tragedies. The pattern of storyline introduces us to a character that is pursuing integrity yet is overcome by their own character defects which go unrecognized. When they finally realize the depths of their challenges, it is usually too late. Edwards Dowdan, a 19th century literacy reviewer theorized how "Tragedy as conceived by Shakespeare is concerned with the ruin or restoration of the soul and of the life of man." So, the question becomes: Are we able to recognize our temptations and sins before it leads to our destruction?

I am certainly not insinuating that our character defects are the reason we experience human suffering, but I am asking you to reflect on your own patterns in order to intervene with the prolonging of your suffering. For example, maybe you did make significant mistakes in a friendship that led to the end of a relationship. Relationships are two ways, and the longer you allow shame to keep you closed off from the world, the longer we prolong our suffering.

The apostle Paul wrote a letter to the city of Corinth which has been shared with us as the book of Romans, which is the sixth book of the New Testament. Paul proclaims:

> "Not only so, but we also glory in our sufferings, because we know that suffering produces perseverance; perseverance, character; and character, hope. And hope does not put us to shame, because God's love has been poured out into our hearts through the Holy Spirit, who has been given to us."

Suffering is inevitable. Suffering produces resilience and strength.

I often use the analogy of a car dashboard when I am teaching my clients about emotional identification. Now if you are anything like me, I am not so automobile savvy. If my engine light happens to come on, I generally think "Ooooh that's not good", but I certainly could not tell you what it means. Our emotional signals are similar. If I experience a fit of rage, my immediate thought is "this is strong". When we work towards distress tolerance, we become less controlled by our emotional experience, and more able to respond in an appropriate manner. Another confusing element to emotional regulation is making sense of how we can feel multiple emotions co currently. We must understand how to identify, process, and regulate the emotions we experience.

Apathy: The Unassuming Guest

As we have already discussed, we will continuously experience dips, suffering and loss. While it can be natural to become overwhelmed or consumed by this truth, I have noticed how this pattern does not typically lead to developing dreams and pursuing goals. This truth can lead to something dangerous. I am referring to apathy. Apathy is a sneaky visitor that can creep through the front door of our minds unassumingly. If we start to experience this flavor of emotion, I am not suggesting that we devalue its presence. Apathy can stem from ideas and thoughts such as "never getting to where we want to be" or that "life will continue to disappoint us".

From Apathy to Activated Life

So maybe you resonate with the idea of an apathetic mindset, and I want to encourage you with ideas of how to overcome this stuck-ness. Apathy tends to result from doing the same thing over and over. I am sure you might have heard the quote "Doing the same thing over and over and expecting a different result is the definition of insanity." So, what is the next step to overcoming apathy? I would argue that it lies within the title of this book.

Simply Beginning. We want to work towards noting our apathy and acting as a result.

Looking to the word of God, the Bible uses the phrase "hardening of the heart" in many of the stories and parables. Let's start with Ephesians 4:18:

> "They are darkened in their understanding and separated from the life of God because of the ignorance that is in them due to the hardening of their hearts."

Proverbs 28:14 states:

> "Blessed is the one who always trembles before God, but whoever hardens their heart falls into trouble."

From a modern perspective, I am intrigued how a "hardened heart" translates into our current cultural climate. I also recognize that this is a book that is being written in 2023. I can only hope these ideas translate to years beyond this moment. Using the biblical understanding of this concept, I studied what characteristics and patterns led to a "hardening of the heart". From Biblical reference, I noted how things like pride and arrogance were key contributors to the hardening of Pharaoh's heart. Another familiar theme of this concept exists within moments of extreme disappointment and grief. It is inevitable that human experience is a life of gifts, but also a wealth of trials. When we start to lose our spirit, we fall into pits of despair that can feel impossible to crawl out of entirely. If we can start to view disappointments and trials as opportunities for new life, this can aid the process of softening our hearts both towards others as well as ourselves.

I dare you to find a time of suffering in your life that you feel destroyed you. The fact of the matter is that you are reading this book. To me, that displays a hope and curiosity that your future could feel less empty and more aligned with what you know and believe to be important. Time and time again we face trials, and time and time again, we could start to restore the brokenness we experience as a part of our humanness.

So, if a hardening of the heart is generally stimulated by our own temptations, sins, and distorted cognitions, are we able to start to express compassion and also keep ourselves accountable to use this knowledge to move towards our calling?

Below is a list of "the seven deadly sins". I do want to iterate that there are more than 7 types of sin, but I appreciate this list because I feel that it encompasses many of our more nuanced struggles. For example, if I spend inappropriate time on my social media presence rather than my present relationships, it is possible that I struggle with pride. This exploration is not meant to simply point out your character flaws. In fact, I believe that you are a dynamic human with plenty of opportunity to choose dark or light, but I would be remiss if I did not believe that we are all uniquely tempted. Take a moment to review the options and engage in a bit of expressive writing around how these characteristics may be contributors towards your internal struggles:

1. Pride

2. Greed

3. Lust

4. Anger

5. Gluttony

6. Envy

7. Sloth

As a psychotherapist, this book is not directed towards those who are experiencing clinical depression, although through my treatment approach, I tend to use many similar tools. Take for example "Opposite Actions". This is a tool and skill that comes from Dialectical Behavioral Therapy, and this specific strategy has been a game changer for many of the clients with whom I have worked in the past[1]. Opposite actions teach the skill as a practice as the name suggests. For example, if we biologically feel anger, what might it be like to respond with empathy and compassion? I know this sounds unnatural, but changing our response does hold the opportunity to elicit a different result.

1. See Recommended Reading

If we were to take this a step further, let's think about your stuckness. What emotions are coupled with your tendency to freeze or withdraw from taking steps towards your goals? If you experience bouts of shame, what might it be like to respond with a regulated tone, make eye contact, and exercise confidence? Fear can cause us to want to retract into our turtle shell. What would it take to keep pursuing your goals and build resilience?

In the section below, I would like you to identify what emotions you feel are getting in the way of achieving steps towards your vision. If you want to write a book, maybe the feeling of inadequacy is at work in your mind. If you want to start to exercise more, maybe the feeling of dread is a barrier. Here is the thing. Emotions are true, but they do not always equate to the truth of our realities. So take some time to explore this for yourself. I may feel inferior as a mom, but that does not mean this is true. Write out your emotional blockages below:

____

____

____

____

____

____

Reflective Pause:

I am aware that my experience is going to be entirely different and unique to others that are on this road to transformation. That said, I do want to be honest about my process as I continue to mold this manuscript into what I hope it will become, and what I KNOW it will become. As I have stuck with the process, I feel as if I am gaining traction in a positive, hopeful way. I feel as if I finally have a lot of the ideas that have been swirling around in my head written down, and now the journey is to organize the ideas and expand upon them to provide applicable tools to my readers. I share all of this to encourage you to stick with the process that you are committing to achieving. Yes, it will be messy. Yes, it will be uncertain. But if we are aware of these truths, we can expect the process to be unlike anything we could have imagined. Stick with it!

Chapter 7: Highlight the Resilience,
Have Compassion for the Human

We are not always taught how to accept and take responsibility for our role in the world. We are a blend of noble, positive human characteristics and gifts, and we are all drawn to unique ways of straying from our paths. Our path can only be dictated by what or whom we allow to lead our moral compass. Now if we do not abide by a moral compass, we can tend to feel lost and frustrated that our own value system seems to be leaving us in a mess of confusion. I personally derive my moral compass from my faith, and I understand that this is not the case for everyone. Maybe you generate your moral compass from politics or Hollywood. Maybe you have created your ideals based off your families or your partners. I would highly encourage you to complete the values assessment, as well as ask yourself why these domains *are* important to you. For example, if I choose integrity as one of my values, it might stem from my worldly belief that honesty and leadership are important to my experience.

I am simply asking you to take a long hard look in the mirror, and to clearly articulate what you see reflecting. This is the only possible way to truly deepen your relationship with your spirit today. To me, there is no point in putting off this union. If we allow another responsibility to get in the way of the deepening of this relationship, it is possible that you will find yourself on a never-ending loop of allowing your circumstances to dictate your values rather than your heart. To me, that is one cause of the loss of so many incredible stories. When a human being surrenders their spirit and values to the world, their unique perspective, potential ideas, and wisdom are relinquished. Yet, if we can acknowledge the difficult nature of human experience, we can start to comprehend the deep suffering that lies within every human heart to better understand ourselves. How many times have you seen the advice, "be your own person, be yourself, never change for another person . . . " Blah blah blah. Sure, I agree with these concepts to a certain extent, but what if I were to tell you that my "true self" exists within the gray area. These are where the controversial themes of life come into play. And these contain deeply difficult ideas and philosophies. These are the corner spaces where we must turn to our higher power or system of belief to try to process for ourselves. And if you are anything like me, there are several things that I certainly do not believe to be black and white, and there are some concepts that I may never fully work out for myself. But I also can walk in peace knowing that having a certain, surefire answer will not solve the pain of whatever circumstance I am wrestling with, and my job is simple and straightforward. I believe my job is to accept and love others. I believe that it is a calling to listen to the stories of others, and provide them with support, reflection, encouragement, and hope. We can empathize with others, but we can never fully experience their stories apart from what they share.

While this book is inspired to provide you with encouragement and skills, I do feel a calling to step into territory that may not look so pretty on the outside. Working at the yoga studio, I was introduced to a lovely human named Maurice who exuded kindness and stories. He framed our internal dialogue to that of "our closest roommate" and emphasized that we should treat ourselves with dignity, respect, and love. I believe that this is an integral step to better understand ourselves, our behavior, and how we can start to shift the narrative we have with our "closest roommate". I believe for a fact that every human has circumstances in which they wish they could have done things differently. To be frank, this is the nature of human experience. Where I have observed clients, friends, and my-self getting stuck is when we choose to hang onto all the moments we regret and internalize them as a part of our character. Enter shame. When we are stuck in storms of shame, we are physically unable to move anywhere. Sometimes we try to outrun the shame storm by being as busy as we possibly can to avoid the incoming waves of regret that pierce our character and our hearts. Sometimes we try to rationalize or defend our stories because we have the luxury of knowing the finite details of our challenges. While our pain is valid, I am inviting you to start to make peace with all the parts of yourself. The areas you are proud of, but more importantly, the areas in which you feel the sting of shame.

Psalm 51:10 asks the Lord to:

> "Create in me a pure heart, O God, and renew a steadfast
> spirit within me."

What amazes me about my God is that he has forgiven us before we even act. He only asks us to ask Him for forgiveness. My God is in the business of healing, and I do not believe that He has created us to live in the horrors of our pasts or self-narratives. He encourages us to move forward with grace. We will all face trials. Some from the hand of others, and commonly at the hand of ourselves. We are not meant to live in this space. We can start to clean up our mess by asking for forgiveness and renewal of the heart. Have you ever apologized to someone, but still felt like that apology was not enough to move past the shame of what you have done? This is an opportunity to trade shame for conviction. If we can learn from our mistakes, ask for accountability for our actions, and move forward with a renewed heart, we can start to shift the narratives from "You are a horrible person" to "You made some mistakes, and you can learn from your humanness."

As a psychotherapist, I believe shame is conditioned, and my clients are frequently unaware of when it rears its sneaky head because it has become such a normalized experience. Like any emotion, shame has a role. Shame is important to recognize. Romans 12:4-5 conveys:

> "For just as each of us has one body with many members, and these members do not all have the same function, so in Christ we, though many, form one body, and each member belongs to all the others."

We are designed to experience the gamut of emotional experience. I often use "an emotion wheel" to help my clients understand the diversity of emotions. To make it even more confusing, we generally experience multiple emotions simultaneously, so the art of identifying them is not always clear and straightforward. For example, several years back, I left a job that I loved because my family was relocating. While I was hopeful and excited about the season to come, I also felt a sharp sting of loss as I navigated terminating professional relationships that I had come to know, count on, and love.

Shame plays a role, but unless we can understand when we are experiencing the storm, we may struggle to find a way out, leaving us feeling powerless, and stuck. Only recently have I begun to fully become aware of when I find myself in my own shame storms, which has been a quite liberating experience. If we know what is happening within us, it sets us up to be able to weather the storm and regulate to a place of centeredness.

I want to get a little personal for a moment. While I understand that shame presents differently for everyone, I want to share my experience to help you to identify what shame may look and feel like in your own mind and body.

Shame starts to sneak in when I am triggered by the thought that I do not belong. When I begin to question where I am in any given season of my life, I can start to raise awareness around where shame might be lurking around the corner. If you are anything like me, and I am assuming you are in some way because we are all human, one negative cognition can lead to a spiral or domino effect of shame-based beliefs and ideas. Often this happens when I am experiencing imposter syndrome, or when I am surrounded by individuals who I perceive to be different than me. So different in fact, that I feel there is not space available for me. Physically, I notice my body starting to become rigid and closed off. I may cross my legs, or arms to become a smaller version of myself. I begin to become less present because I am allowing myself to get swept away by the waves of my mind. As I allow the thoughts and questions, my stress and anxiety start to escalate. Instead of noting what is happening, sometimes I start to ask questions to the people around to either affirm or negate my sense of belonging. The tricky part is, no matter what their response is, I use this as ammo to fuel my shame tank. It is only when I can acknowledge the shame within myself that I am able to take steps to de-escalate and remind myself of truths. To put things in perspective, in the past, my shame storms often ended in uncontrollable tears, fits of rage, and sabotaging the relationships around me. As you can imagine, this is a destructive pattern towards the health of my relationships. This is destructive because I invalidate all the accompanying emotions and allow shame to become the driver of my actions and thoughts. Shame becomes in control.

Building resilience is a process, and it is not something that we are born with. Resilience is an earned state of mind. We cannot understand resilience until we have waded through the waters of failure and disappointment. If we can learn to use our shame storms, rather than letting them consume us, we are able to gather the strength and power to overcome our human nature and become more like the incredibly strong individuals that I believe God designed us to be in the first place. I offer these ideas to empower you to learn. I offer these notions to empower you to feel. If you can start to become more in tune with all the parts of yourself, you then hold the key to moving into the next season of your life with a strength that cannot be purchased. I do not believe human beings are born resilient, but I do believe that human beings all possess the power to make meaningful changes in their own lives regardless of circumstances. It does take a certain level of emotional intelligence and awareness, which I also understand are not available resources for all. With that said, you hold a very powerful role with your own knowledge. While inequality is pervasive and true, individuals with access to greater resources can help to facilitate a culture of shame resilience. Before we move into how you can actively participate in the war against shame storms, I do want you to take personal time to better identify what and how your shame storms may look like. I want you to stay alert because the clutches of shame are strong, and sometimes just recounting times when you may have been in a storm can open the floodgates to experience it again. And if we are self-aware, you now know that you do not have to give into these human tendencies.

Shame promotes the idea that our character is somehow broken and flawed. Have you ever felt like you wanted to somehow become as small as possible in any given situation? You may feel as if you are frozen in time and would do anything to retreat from the circumstance in which you find yourself. Shame is a normal human occurrence, and we are not meant to stay in this space. Shame can eat away at our sense of self, which cuts us off from not only knowing our strengths and gifts, but not having time and space to even begin to tap into these gifts.

I may sound like a broken record, but I so desperately want you to build up your tool kit to reduce *prolonged* shame. It is important to recognize that if we internalize shame through our childhood and development, it can be a strange notion to start to recognize that staying in a shame-based mindset is not a healthy state of being. Shame based parenting can often lead to trouble with shame into adulthood. Discipline and shame are not equal. Additionally, if you are anything like me, you understand that we are not typically taught how to emotionally regulate in grade school, or even the purpose of complex emotions. Think about this information as a new beginning. Our culture has certainly begun to truly recognize the importance of tending to our mental health, which is wonderful, and there are also so many conflicting ideas about the best ways to approach this task. I believe that this is an individualized approach to every person. Just like we all have our unique stories, there are unique ways to formulate a plan for forward progression. If therapy was a one size fits all approach, sure you might gain some nuggets of information, but it would take a lot of tailoring to truly find the healing that your body and mind are asking of you. With this idea in mind, I also believe there are general ways that we can start to broach these topics. The first step starts with acknowledging your emotional experience within your mind, heart, body, and spirit. If I know what I am feeling, I can articulate it better. I can then ask for support or use coping skills to help me regulate intense emotions. Think about a time when you were in a new city for the first time. You may be using google maps, but you are unsure of your territory, and can even feel quite lost. You do not know where the gas stations are located, or where to find the grocery store. Once you start to familiarize yourself with your surroundings, you begin to function, and usually flourish. A new map can be transformed into a home, where you start to thrive. You find your favorite food spots and know where to locate friends. I believe the same to be true about our emotional experience. If we are unfamiliar with the process, it can certainly feel bleak or overwhelming. Once we start the process of familiarizing ourselves, we can start to become friends with our emotions. Once we are established within ourselves, only then can we thrive.

Chapter 8: Your Transformation

Although we likely do not know one another personally, we have been able to cultivate a meaningful relationship through language. You have probably gotten a sense of who I am and how I think, or you might not still be reading this book. You also trust me enough to continue thinking about the ideas that I am presenting, and for that I am grateful. As your new friend, I can only imagine the hands and minds that this text may reach one day, and can I just start by saying how excited I am for you?

What initially led me to ask the same questions that you are asking of yourself is what led me to writing a book.

We tend to prioritize what we are comfortable with doing, or not doing for that matter. Of course, there are adult responsibilities that cause us to spend entirely too much time focusing on our jobs and careers, but what if we were to dedicate more time prioritizing creative ways of integrating our passions and callings into our "have tos". I am certainly not asking you to work more, but I am asking you to rethink why and how you have landed where you are today. Many individuals truly limit their abilities simply because they do not believe in themselves enough to take risks.

And again, I have been guilty of this myself many times. Everyone has their own version of "busy". We work jobs, sustain family units, take care of pets, take care of our spaces, try to contribute to the community . . . the list could easily go on and on. But we must also take accountability for not prioritizing things that we desire to explore. For example, this has happened time and time again as I navigate writing this book. I allow myself to continually make excuses for why I didn't get a chance to write day to day, and the excuses are valid. I do work a 40+ hour work week. I am also pursuing my PhD, running my business, and prioritizing my family and my marriage. And of course, where does that leave my dedication to my faith? I have only recently truly begun to understand my faith as something that has to be integrated rather than checked off a to do list. Like any relationship we experience as a human, there are days when I realize that my walk with the Lord is "out of step". If you have ever had a partner, you know this can happen from time to time for plenty of reasons. Sometimes life throws us hailstorms when we are expecting sunshine. Regardless of where the stress comes from, we can become out of sync with one another. The imperative action here is to have a conversation with the person we are feeling distant from to get on the same page again. The beauty of the Christian faith is that the Lord is continually pursuing us, welcoming us back into His arms anytime we come to Him. Yet because of shame, pressure, and a lack of self-love, we can stray or avoid our Father as if he is going to throw the book at us. As if he is going to shame us for getting our priorities jumbled. But the relational nature of our God is entirely the opposite of this. Fleshly relationships may have played a part in your perception that you have to do things perfectly, act with integrity one hundred percent of the time, and be flawless to be deemed "good", but the truth is that you do not have to earn our Father's love, you just have to receive and accept it. And believe in yourself enough to recognize that you were designed for perfect union with your Spirit and with the one who created us all.

An integral piece of the puzzle of holistic living involves inspiration and creation. Time and time again, I have found myself in the therapeutic realm with a client who just feels "stuck" or if they are not contributing to the world in the way they had imagined. Ideally, we tend to romanticize what this might look like. Speaking on big stages, being the home "room mom", or becoming a content creator. But what if I were to offer the idea that your contribution starts in the little steps you take each day to use your voice and spirit. Maya Angelou once said, "I've learned that people will forget what you said. People will forget what you did, but people will never forget how you made them feel."[1] Shift your focus from the big dreams to the day-to-day interactions and choices. Starting small leads to long term impact.

So where does your "transformation "begin? Again, I would argue that you have already started. Reading leads to suggestions, philosophies, and perspectives around how the world functions and operates. This book provides these perspectives from one 31-year-old woman. But true transformation requires a few different concepts that I will outline below. Feel free to disagree, but these items might be good steppingstones to allow you to discern what is next for you.

1. Diversity of Experiences

2. Continued Learning & Evolving

3. Shifting Your Patterns

4. Internal Belief that your story matters

If we are not careful, our gifts and passions can get lost in the mess. I would argue that this does the world a disservice because your story and talents are needed. I would like to circle back to the first notion that I have addressed.

Diversity of Experiences

Throughout my journey, I have been offered the opportunity to work in two of the most diverse cities in America. I have not always remained true to my identity. I mentioned earlier that we must welcome the evolution of ourselves, and that is the truth. In fact, in my younger years, I believe that I was quite moldable which created quite a bit of insecurity in how I navigated the world around me. I have always been a creative individual and drawn to the arts. I

1. Angelou, *Rainbow,* 41.

have also been energized by spirituality. When I had big questions about the world around me, I always felt as if there was a spiritual realm that I could not fully understand. For many years, I assumed there was something missing in my heart that did not allow me to tap into my own spirituality. I internalized this as a personal flaw. Though as I have grown and matured, my spiritual health has also done the same. I confused religion and spirituality. I interpreted religion as something that those around me naturally believed, and as I have come to understand my own faith, I now recognize that my relationship with God is actually very similar to maintaining other healthy relationships in my life. It takes work, dedication, commitment, and the continued feeding of my faith.

Through my venture into the big world around me, I got the chance to witness and hear stories of individuals who have grown up in completely different socio-economic backgrounds and geographic locations, who have sometimes never been exposed to my God. Individuals who have overcome pain and trials that I cannot even begin to fathom or imagine. I remember having significant conversations with my internship supervisor, Danny. As a 23-year-old white female from Texas, I could not understand how I might have anything to offer the individuals of color who have been misdiagnosed, mistreated, and consistently in and out of the legal system in New York City. Danny reminded me that my offering was simply that of my desire to use my talents and skills to share my heart. There was one patient who grew to really act as a protector towards me. Violent outbursts would often happen in the psychiatric forensic unit that I worked on for several months. On my last day, clinicians and patients were sitting in a circle to discuss rules and regulations of the unit when one patient jumped towards another and started violently beating him. When this occurred, the patient who had grown close to me jumped in front of me as a symbol of protection.

I did not deserve this more than any other person in that room, but I took this as a symbol of this man seeing that I did care, and although I could not relate to what their lives had been like, there is humanness in recognizing the heart of others. Working in secular organizations, I have served as a therapist for individuals from different religions, backgrounds, and cultures. I now stand firm in my own identity and recognize that everyone has their own identity. If we can show up as a beacon of love for one another, we can remember that the one thing that we ultimately share is the human experience. I share this to encourage you to spend time with people who are unlike you. There is so much to learn. We are often drawn to what we are comfortable with, but when we enter discomfort with an open heart and mind, we can shine our internal light for others who are experiencing the darkness of this world, and often feel the warmth of their light. There will always be times in our lives when we experience lightness and fullness, and other times when we feel like we cannot even begin to fathom moving or what our next step might look like. No one is immune to hope or suffering, but no matter what, we must help one another along the journey. This is one pivotal reason as to why your experience matters. What your heart longs to do is valid. What your heart longs to achieve is necessary. This has shifted my focus in writing this book from "I cannot do this; I am not an author" to "I must do this. This is my duty as a fellow human". We want to recognize that each human being has a unique story, and we can honor their stories by feeling confident enough to rise and share our own.

Continued Learning and Evolving

Section two ventures into an opportunity that aids in the ability to actively CHOOSE to continue to evolve. I will warn that this can be a tricky venture if we are unsteady in our own identity. If we are unable to accept ourselves for who we are, gaining more information can sometimes exasperate confusion. If we feel confused about our identity, we will feel drawn to many areas of identification, and questioning ourselves can be a painful process. So, I encourage you to tap into your own insight to stand firm in who you are today. Again, we are ever changing, so nothing is set in stone, but we must commit to showing up authentically in who we are *today*. For example, I can still be sure of my identity if I have not fully decided what I want out of life. In fact, the process of living and evolving is precisely what leads to these answers.

The Bible teaches me that I am chosen, saved, sanctified, forgiven, a light, called for good works, made anew each day, sufficient, intricately designed and no longer a slave. These truths are not unique to me. In fact, these truths are available for all who choose to believe. Simply becoming a Christian does not mean that we are immune to the sickness within our human hearts, but by his grace, we are able to extract the poison of our own hearts.

Psalm 139:23-24 states:

> "Search me, God, and know my heart;
> test me and know my anxious thoughts.
> See if there is any offensive way in me,
> and lead me in the way everlasting."

I encourage you to ask the Lord to reveal the pain of your own heart. He will bring your wounds to the surface. This can be a painful process, but necessary for the growth of our new foundation.

As we become renewed, we can start tapping into our holy callings imprinted upon our DNA from the Lord. I do not believe that one must be an expert in one thing to start living into these callings, but I must accept the responsibility that comes along with chasing goals and desires. If I want to open a restaurant one day, it would be impractical to not research everything that goes into venturing into this territory. Maybe you want to express yourself through music, it might be a worthwhile effort to start to learn how to read a scale. It is not always necessary to have the skills. In fact, I think we also have many natural God given abilities and talents. Just because I might have a skill of connecting with someone, as a therapist, I have a duty to study theory and learn interventions to properly conduct the work that I have been called to do.

Learning is a lifelong hobby because it is something that simply does not end. This can be a daunting concept for those of us who thrive on efficiency and production. Finishing a task is satisfying, yet learning is a lifelong practice. If we adopt certain maladaptive behaviors, yet do not learn from them, we will continue to find ourselves stuck. I want to offer an idea that may sound simple but can certainly progress your creative thinking. If you are stuck in a particular area of your life, why not research other individuals who have gone through similar experiences?

A part of my story was about a life-threatening fight with anorexia. Before I had enough insight into what was happening to my body, both psychologically and biologically, the patterns made sense to me. Sadly, it was only when my body started to stop functioning that I recognized the severity of my maladaptive patterns. While this is a big example, there are most likely daily rhythms that are holding you back from entering the next chapter of life. Take time to reveal these for yourself. Treat yourself with the greatest care and compassion and recognize your power to move forward.

Shifting Your Patterns

We have discussed how easy it can feel to become trapped in the patterns of everyday life and attend to our jobs and the needs of others. I have recognized how common it can also become for individuals to lose themselves in the process.

I had dinner with my girlfriend tonight. We were chatting about a text that I had sent earlier in the day that read "if you feel over extended, we can always do dinner on a different night." She responded with so much enthusiasm that we *were* in fact holding on to our commitment, and I couldn't help but smile. We had an in-depth conversation about how easy it is to not do meaningful things, something as simple as having dinner together. And can I tell you how incredibly inspired I feel after making the effort to simply spend time with a friend exploring a new restaurant with our dogs? While this is a simple example, think about all the ideas that get thrown to the curb because of our own excuses. "How will I ever find time?" Or "I wouldn't even know where to start." That right there is the message that I feel called to share with this book. The first step to achieving anything, be that a dinner date with a friend or your biggest dreams start with *simply beginning.*

Internal Belief that your Story Matters

Confidence is something that we develop, I personally do not believe that confidence is a natural gift. Pride, on the other hand, can easily be confused with high self-esteem. It is important to be able to discern the difference, both for us and how we assess the character of those around us. High levels of self-confidence have been associated with a strong sense of personal worth and belief, the tendency towards generosity rather than compassion and high levels of instinctual humility. Pride generally manifests from the exact opposite- insecurity, envy, and dissatisfaction. The two can often be confused, but I do encourage you to use your internal compass to decipher the character of your own heart as well as others.

Proverbs 11:2 states:

> "When pride comes, then comes disgrace, but with humility comes wisdom."

It breaks my heart to experience clients in my life who struggle with their sense of self because of how someone in their life has treated them. I have also made this error many times in my past, which has led me down a confusing and winding path. If you personally feel like you are lacking purpose in your life, I invite you to explore whether someone in your life may be getting in the way of your forward progression, or is it simply yourself? I would venture to guess that it is a mix of the two. We condition ourselves to believe we are only capable of meeting certain milestones because of our circumstances and internal belief system. Certainly, there are a myriad of different obstacles for different individuals, but we are also designed for resilience and growth. What if you were to lift the weight of the restraints that you feel hold you back from moving forward? I am not conveying that we will not face severe challenges as we persist, in fact that is a part of the journey, but I am articulating that your lack of esteem in yourself might be the first hurdle to plunge towards.

Let's try another creative exercise. This is an expressive writing or flow of conscious thought. Feel free to write down everything you can think of in a span of three minutes or record yourself answering the prompt below. This exercise will serve as a gateway to release data regarding your self-esteem, and what you believe you can achieve in your core:

Set timer for 3 minutes, and answer prompt below:

> *If money and status were not a part of the equation, and you could take a year to explore anything in your life, what would you want or choose to do?*

Now that you have completed the assignment, take three minutes to re-read your answers or listen back to your recording. Ask yourself if this was a difficult question. Did your answers feel realistic? Did they feel hindered by circumstances? I want you to try this again, but I want you to dig deeper. Cultivate the heart of a child. I want you to dream *bigger*! There is no one here to judge you. If nothing else, this is an exercise of playfulness and creativity. Dig deeper for yourself. Dig deeper for the world. Our dreams can no longer be limited by the structural and financial limitations of our organized society.

I am here to tell you that you, *yes you*, can create amazing things, and they stem from your story. All it takes is the next right step in the direction of the picture you can create in your mind. So maybe you want to generate kindness globally? Sure, that is a big dream, and that is *exactly* the passion that we need to get you on the right path. That is an example of your heart shining through the fragmented constraints of this manufactured world that we live within. The privilege of living in America is access to opportunity. I do hope that this book is a vehicle to reach outside of our corner of the world, but this is a friendly reminder to my fellow Americans that we live in a culture of privilege and opportunity. Certainly, there is generational trauma and disproportionate resources allocated (unfortunately) to certain demographics, but you are also the key to breaking the cracks.

Reflective Pause:

I must be honest and say that I took several days off writing. I initially felt guilty, but then comforted myself due to my full caseload at work. I can certainly have compassion for myself, but I also have a goal and a duty. What has helped my process is having smaller goals. For example, in my calendar, every two weeks, I have a page limit goal that I am attempting to reach to get my ideas out on paper. Would you believe that it is working? While I am short of the goal that I had initially set for this Saturday, the day is only getting started. I have found that time and time again, we must encourage ourselves and light the fire. *Otherwise, we remain the same.* This is a pivotal moment in this writing journey to allow the rest of this text to fall to the wayside like so many of my other projects, but this project is not my others. This book is important to me because I have a message to share. And even deeper, I feel as if this message is from the Lord, not myself. I am simply his vessel. I am His tool to use in whatever way He needs me. I am not thinking ahead, I am not editing as I go, I am simply in the depths of this journey. I have moved past simply beginning into the deep layers of the forest of opportunity. It is uncertain. Sometimes it can feel cold, or I might feel lost, and I know where my internal compass is leading me, so I choose to continue the path with a trust in myself that I will reach the ambiguous destination, and once I am there, it will be the beginning of a brand-new journey. I encourage you as my reader, do not stop now. The path ahead grants the map to deciphering what is on your heart, how to express it, and how to recognize fear in its tracks. I believe so many good works will come from sharing your story, and I cannot wait for the world to experience what you want to offer.

Chapter 9: Brainstorm, Cultivate, Create

This chapter will embrace spontaneity to help you decipher what is important to you, and what is in your heart to share with the world. We all have unique ways of processing and coping with the events life throws at us. For next week, I have a challenge for you. This challenge will surely be a mental test, but I also wonder what it might help you reveal about your person. I would never ask you to try something that I am unwilling to attempt myself. I also would not offer this idea if I did not truly believe in its power. For the next seven days, the challenge is to significantly reduce stimulation and technology. Why am I asking you this? We live in a generation where most of the population admits "not knowing how to relax". Often when I ask clients what they do for fun, they report watching television shows with their partners to "wind down". The amount of times Netflix comes before the option to pick up a book makes me sick to my stomach. That said, I am an artist, and there are reasons we are drawn to movies and television. I would argue that the biggest draw is the opportunity to disconnect from us, and fantasize about fictional characters, and witness their stories. As a drama therapist, I very much believe in the power of storytelling and aesthetic distance, but I also wonder if the excess of stimulation is cutting us off from processing our own life. Think about it. When you arise in the morning, you are met with hundreds of small choices and decisions you will navigate as you enter the day. There is no day that is the same, and there are important moments in each day that shape our perception of the world. Now, we do not usually have the privilege of processing life events as they happen. No, we must move on with our day. That is why I believe the end of your day may be one of the most important moments, as we are offered the chance to reflect on what happened and how we are feeling. From there, we have an important task to decide the best ways to care for ourselves and recharge our batteries for the day ahead. If we fall into routines that are too strict, we will experience the comfort of knowing what to expect, but I am positing that these strict routines do not usually leave space to process and express ourselves. This is my theory behind this challenge. I encourage you to slow your evenings down and listen to what your body and mind are sharing with you. Maybe making dinner rather than picking up takeout would be a nourishing choice. What if your body is asking for a hot shower or to simply put lotion on your joints for the first time in months? We create patterns of coping with the stress of our everyday lives, and I am asking for you to rethink your patterns. Without the distraction of media and technology, how do you take care of yourself and how do you process the ever-changing winds of your story?

Feel free to take notes to write any reflections or insights that you gain as you navigate the next week. Maybe you use journaling as a form of daily processing. What a perfect expression of mindfulness and intentionality. Whether you decide to journal daily, or simply express how you feel about the exercise, I can promise that you will learn *something*. Maybe your conclusions at the end of the week do not align with mine, and that is okay as well. You know yourself and your body better than anyone, but why not give yourself the opportunity to try?

I would posit that a significant reduction in technology and distraction has left you with ample time for your mind to wander, but worse, to worry. We want to utilize and steward the resources we must create a "complete and full life for ourselves". In fact, God has the same desires.

John 10:10 states:

> "The thief comes only to steal and kill and destroy; I have
> come that they may have life and have it to the full."

I believe that God has created you to fulfill your unique purpose to redeem this world that is infiltrated with trials and suffering. Each one of us has a unique story, and we develop interests and passions along the way. I wonder what would happen if you began to surrender your pressure to figure it all out and allow the Good Shepherd to guide you along the way. The truth is every answer you need to start this journey is already within you and your heart. I also believe that it takes a certain level of trust and surrender to believe this for yourself. My challenge is that we start to remove the weeds and distractions and allow the Holy Spirit to energize your heart to recognize what you already know.

As we begin to shed distractions, I understand that this may feel like a vulnerable and confusing place to be left. Without world attention, we have time to reveal the writings in our heart and use our own judgment to decide what to do with that information.

Now that we have ventured into the idea of shedding the hypnotic nature of technology, I would like you to ask yourself what else might be serving as a distraction and removing you from accessing your heart and your callings. Distractions can take many forms. In fact, they can even be noble causes that are important to you, but if they are taking the space needed to look inwards, they might be holding you back from what you *need to recognize*. I have shared this before, and I stand by my testimony that a life of busyness may in fact be taking you on a journey of prolonged distraction from sharing your true gifts with the world. Of course, this is a gray area, but it can certainly be a difficult pattern to recognize and start to untangle. Take for example the story of Martha and Mary when they were in Jesus' presence. In the story, Martha was running about her house trying to perfect dinner and clean. Does this sound familiar? Mary, on the other hand, was at the feet of Jesus, spending time with him and being present. Jesus responds to this with the verse below. Luke 10:41-42 states:

"Martha, Martha," the Lord answered, "you are worried and upset about many things, but few things are needed—or indeed only one. Mary has chosen what is better, and it will not be taken away from her."

It blew my mind when I personally recognized how many of my noble feats truly served to distract me from the weight of my soul and my story. I found drama to be healing through my mother's assault and recovery, and for ten years, I used theater as a means of escapism. The theater provided everything for me wrapped up in a pretty bow. Auditions were challenging, rejection was difficult, and I learned to cope with over time. Getting the call that I had been cast gave me the validation that I was worthy of being a part of something important, and meeting fellow cast members was like entering high school for the first time. I instantly assessed who I clicked with, and began to learn the unique qualities, stories and needs of each of my colleague cast members. We would devise a story together. That story would include dance, song, and strong emotional moments. Then we would add elements like costumes and set pieces to continue to establish our new world together. Opening night would hit and we would perform from our hearts to draw the audience into our intimate work of art. As you can imagine, theater has held space for me to stay busy and to move outside of my own life, into a different reality and world. Coping with reality and the world can be exhausting, and this outlet provided me space to breathe. And while I am certainly not demonizing theater, I did so many shows throughout my college years, I never took time to reflect on my own world or troubles.

My hope is that you find similar qualities that align with your own interests. It may not be as time consuming, or as adventurous as my theater exploration, but I do hope and pray that you find outlets that allow you to play and breathe. Time and time again, the arts have been understood to improve the wellbeing of mental health. Creativity and spontaneity allow us to engage in active problem solving as well as simply having fun. The next assessment we will explore will hopefully help you to decipher what forms of creativity speak to your personal interests and allow you to build up your toolbox of skills that allow you to breathe and maybe even . . . . Have some fun. If you ever feel like there is something missing, my guess is that there are layers of your story and experience that are begging to be seen and expressed. It is possible that creativity can help to serve as a vehicle for these longings.

Below, you will find another assessment. The mission is simple, I would like you to circle or highlight items that stand out to you. There is no right or wrong way to complete this assessment, it is just meant to give us some insight into your personality and gifts.

Modalities of Creativity

- Animation
- Antiques
- Baking
- Blogging
- Bullet Journaling
- Bucket List Collage
- Collecting
- Coloring
- Comedy Shows
- Cooking
- Dollhouse Creation
- Doodling
- Drawing
- Fashion
- Flower Arrangement
- Furniture Building
- Gardening
- Ghostwriting
- Greeting Card Creation
- Graffiti
- Hiking
- Improvisation

- Jewelry Making
- Knitting
- Libraries
- Make Up
- Movies
- Music
- Nature Exploration
- Painting
- Performance Art
- Photography
- Poetry
- Pottery
- Redecorating
- Scrapbooking
- Sculpting
- Singing
- Sketching
- Videography
- Vision Boarding
- Wall Painting
- Watercolors
- Writing

Now I do not intend for this list to overwhelm you. It has been designed to help guide you in honing in on your unique interests. Your transformation is sure to bring new opportunities and rhythms of renewal into your life, and the journey to this new road may require the art of simplification and trial and error. I urge you to examine your schedule and truly get a good idea of whether your responsibilities are self-imposed. You might be the first person truly getting in the way of deepening your relationship with yourself, and most importantly, with your spiritual health and relationship. The good news is that this is not an end, all be all. In fact, I believe that this is an opportunity. This is opening a new door to increased awareness about the agency you hold in your life.

We all have scars, we all have lived experiences, and each of us experiences emotions such as shame, regret, guilt, and abuse towards ourselves as we have discussed. It is my hope for you to breathe and surrender your fear. We often feel the most authentic and connected when we feel understood by another. I encourage you to celebrate this opportunity to go deep into your relationship with yourself, and with the Lord. Although it may feel messy and uncomfortable, you only risk denying yourself love, compassion and respect. Beyond this, I believe that our Lord is the great physician. He can give us the agency to heal our own wounds, and seek the resources, community, and support to help us along the way.

The verse I am about to share halted me in my tracks. As a Christian and follower of Jesus, I have a sinful tendency of surrendering my mind and body to God, and then allowing the world to knock me off my own path. While I do not condone this pattern, I do want to normalize it for you. We are naturally swayed to feel ourselves pulled in opposing directions, and the world can be a nasty place. I have also found that my own spiritual discipline is what allows me to truly see the cracks in my own heart. There is immense power in recognizing your sinful tendencies and making conscious choices to move in the direction of righteousness vs. worldly favor. Although this may be difficult, even in small doses, the final effects of living a life of spiritual integrity are invaluable. Once you start to heal your broken spaces, you may start to feel the confidence to stand firm in the person you are becoming, not the person you have outgrown. This is not easy, and this is a true transformation. This verse comes from our "holy callings" found in 2 Timothy 1:6-14.

> "For this reason, I remind you to fan into flame the gift of God, which is in you through the laying on of my hands. For the Spirit God gave us does not make us timid, but gives us power, love, and self-discipline. So do not be ashamed of the testimony about our Lord or of me his prisoner. Rather, join with me in suffering for the gospel, by the power of God. He has saved us and called us to a holy life—not because of anything we have done but because of his own purpose and grace."

Reflective Pause:

I am astounded by my own insights, personal growth, and curiosity as I continue this process. I am feeling stronger, mentally, and physically. My self-esteem has grown. Not because I wrote something profound, but because I am following through on a dream of mine. It is possible that this book will miss the mark entirely. It is certainly possible that it will "flop" for lack of better words, but the personal growth that I have experienced through the process is priceless for me, personally. I can only hope that my own experience leads you to act on your own goals, hopes, dreams; I am a writer. I am an author. I am a missionary.

While I am honored that you are taking the opportunity to read this book, and to get to know me as a friend, I am more excited to see what you will start to do after reading this book. We have reviewed the countless reasons as to why we tend to get stuck and refrain from making meaningful steps in our journey. Now I want to explore what to do with this information. The goal is simple. I want you to begin. In whatever way that looks like to you personally. No beginning will look the same, and that is the incredible nature of being human. There are roughly eight billion souls walking this planet, and yet each of our stories are unique. Each of our stories holds meaning, and each of our souls possess the ability to influence change and create something new in this world. What happens next is up to you. You can take a loving, compassionate look in the mirror and begin to dream again. The fact of the matter is that your brain is an incredible organ. The health of your brain is determined by the decisions you make and the thoughts that you believe and meditate on daily. We simply cannot harness the power of our brains and ideas if we are medicating our souls through the means of worldly vices and distractions. I can assume that most individuals want to feel "healed". In fact, I cannot imagine that one of the patients that I work with everyday actively chooses to fall into a life of overwhelming anxiety and deep depression. On a general basis, humans want to feel safe, loved, connected, and hopeful. I would venture to argue that the state of our world does not warrant this desire to be an easy accomplishment. Moreover, each person has extremely different genetic wiring and conditioning. This adds a complex layer because a goal that might be easily obtainable for a privileged, educated, white individual like me may feel out of the question for others. This is muddy water, because it is true that inequality and a lack of justice exist within our world and culture because we try to operate based off manmade politics and governments. I want to encourage you from a place of righteousness rather than our secular constructs. God designed our minds, brains, bodies, and souls based on His own image of perfection. When we were offered the opportunity to divert off our path, sin entered the world, creating mass destruction. We each have a choice. We can give into our own natural stuckness, or we can persevere in the name of what the world needs. With confidence, I want to remind you that the world needs *you*. Just as you are today. Sure, we are all on the journey of bettering ourselves, and healing, in whatever way that looks like, and we are in desperate need of each one of us to hone in on our gifts. If we can even begin to start to tap into the potential that our soul possesses, we will start to feel the impact of realizing more beauty in our world.

You might be thinking, "these are all great ideas, but I do not think they pertain to me. My life is so busy, I am just struggling to pay the bills or make sure the kids are fed." Quite frankly, the busier your life seems, the more I believe this book pertains specifically to you. On the flip side, maybe you feel like you are at a standstill in your life. Each day is just going through the motions, and you feel a sense of apathy when it comes to your future. This book also pertains to you. I hope that you are starting to recognize that this process is meant for anyone willing to venture into uncertainty. I do not believe that there is anything that can truly be lost by taking a chance. Each path taken in life has something to offer us. It may look like the idealistic image of what you expect your dreams to look like. Sometimes rejection is an integral teacher.

When I lived in Houston, I was opening my own private practice. As someone who has always loved collaboration, both personally and professionally, I had a vision of offering a "grand opening celebration". I spent hours researching and inviting therapists across Houston to attend. My vision was that we would have an opportunity to meet, develop connections for a referral base, and start a community of women in the helping profession. I invited over 50 counselors, social workers, and industry professionals. Surprisingly, I received 30 RSVPs for my event. I rented a local yoga studio, bought cupcakes, printed business cards, and invited local vendors to set up booths at this celebration. When the time came, my friends at the time showed up to support me. Guys, one therapist made an appearance. I remember feeling embarrassed, exposed, and gravely disappointed. I remember my imposter syndrome creeping through the cracks, asking myself if I was a joke.

Sure, maybe it was a faulty marketing strategy. It is possible that RSVPs do not hold as much weight as I believed. We were also navigating a post COVID world. Maybe my expectations were a bit unrealistic. Whatever the case, I had an opportunity to use this experience to learn from or to remain stuck and defeated. As I had time to process, I learned several things. I knew that my intentions were aligned with my values, I was proud that I did the best that I could have done with what I knew at the time. I understood that time is our greatest resource. How we choose to spend that time marks a result of what we are prioritizing in our lives. It is certainly possible that these individuals were not in the process of building their practices. It is also possible that they did not fully understand the intention of my event. I chose to learn from this experience, find gratitude for the people in my life who were there to support me, and to embrace the integrity of my dreams even if this method was "unsuccessful" from the lens of my own idealistic expectations. I offer this example to show you that rejection, perceived failures, and unmet expectations are integral steppingstones on your path to purpose. If everything worked the first go around, there would be no journey, therefore the destination would not feel near as rewarding.

When I worked at The Menninger Clinic, I worked with a recovery specialist named Valerie. Val, if you ever come across this book, I hope you know that words simply do not do justice to the impact you had on my life, both as a professional and as a friend. Valerie used to use a quote that has stuck with me for many years. She would say "self-esteem comes from doing esteem able things". The longer that we allow ourselves to stay stuck, or to stay stagnant to avoid rejection or failure, the less we will be able to tap into the creative hope for our future, and for the future of whatever we find meaning within this world. Think about a child trying out for a sports team. In a healthy relationship, a parent is going to be overjoyed for the child to go out and try out. The parent longs for the child to believe in themselves and be patient with the process. Whether or not that child is exponentially gifted in the sport holds no weight. The parent plans to take the child out for pizza to celebrate regardless of the outcome. This is Christ centered encouragement.

1 Thessalonians 5:9-11:

> "For God did not appoint us to suffer wrath but to receive salvation through our Lord Jesus Christ. He died for us so that, whether we are awake or asleep, we may live together with him. Therefore encourage one another and build each other up, just as in fact you are doing."

Christ did not die so that we may put pressure on our children, brothers, and sisters. He died so that this Earth may be redeemed. Note that the verse says, "whether we are awake or asleep, we may live together with him". The fact of the matter is that whether this book "does well" or merits worldly success, I get to live together with Christ. Additionally, I know that I am fulfilling a calling that will (in the best-case scenario) inspire and encourage you to live into yours. We are meant to live fully on the Earth. My hope is that the brokenness of the world will not dictate whether you are "good enough".

With the spirit of encouragement, I want to move us into the "brainstorming" exploration of this chapter. This starts with identifying the places in this world that you feel untethered by the constraints of society, and free to fully show up as an unfiltered version of yourself as a child of God. This sounds welcoming, huh? Make a list of the places in your life that you remember feeling warmly welcomed. Ideally, this would be a place where you find yourself alone in your mind. For myself, I find solace and peace within nature. Funny enough, the first time I recognized what a powerful space this was for me came at a time when I was raking leaves. This was a time in my life where I felt fully under attack by the world and by spiritual warfare. My soul was filled to the brim with anxiety, and the depressive spells came after I felt as if I could not lift my head up. I will never forget that afternoon on a Sunday, in my backyard, raking leaves. My dog rustled around with the leaves, my phone was inside my home, and my soul was opened to the beauty and quiet that surrounded me. I remember wishing I could bottle up this feeling and use it as perfume when uncertainty struck. Recall this place or moment for yourself. If it is a place you can return to, maybe this is a call to take a restorative visit. But also know that this place will be presented differently than it has in the past. The one fact of life is that time continues to tick on, and our lives take new shapes and forms. For many, change can be intimidating. I cannot tell you how many of my clients express to me how much they "hate change". I am here to tell you that change is an integral piece to shaping your story. Change must happen in order for the world to evolve. If we can start to get more comfortable welcoming the change and expecting the change, the uncertainty starts to become less overwhelming.

I also share this safe place idea as a metaphor. Although we may get beaten up by the waves of life, we can always return to this peaceful state of mind. It may not feel simple, easy, or natural, but you do have the capacity to restore. Just like a wound takes time to heal, our bodies, minds and brains are designed to heal. We must pay close attention to what we are feeding ourselves, and what environments we continually return to restore. A beautiful fact of life is that most individuals reading this book have a wide net of autonomy. We may believe we are constrained by the responsibilities and duties of our lives, but what might it feel like to take a day off? I understand that each person has a unique circumstance, but if you are living in a reality where you are constantly pursuing, working, and giving, I do know that you will burn out. This is not a hypothesis. This is scientifically proven. This moment is an opportunity for you to check the battery levels on your heart and mind. Even if you are unable to return to the place of solace and peace that we referenced, close your eyes, and revisit this place in your mind. Take a few breaths to seal the image and see if your body can even imitate what it felt like to be in this space. Once you feel as if you have achieved a level of restoration, we will begin the process of brainstorming.

We have explored countless exercises throughout this text to prime you for this moment. I sometimes teach yoga classes. In my teacher training, we were taught to string poses together that prepare your mind and muscles for a "peak pose". If you have never explored yoga, I encourage you to look up a photo of a "crow pose". This asana is a beautiful integration of wrist strength, core strength, focus, trust, and hip mobility. Even a primed yogi is not going to jump straight into this pose, they are going to practice squats, lunges, and planks to warm up the muscles that are used in the final pose. I use this as a metaphor to acknowledge the fact that you have already done most of the brainstorming work. Throughout this journey, we have identified values, domains and roles of your life, anti-values, your core dreams, and modalities of creativity. Maybe you will take some time to go back and reflect on the journey we have taken together. The answers provided depict the unique qualities of your heart and mind. These are the ingredients we use to prime you for the "peak pose" or the next step of your life practice. In the space provided below, I want you to answer the following prompts. The study for this exam will only be to review the homework you have completed in preparation. When you feel ready, take a breath, remember your space of solace, and proceed forward.

Brainstorm Questionnaire

- What do you understand to be true of the character that you play on Earth?

- How could your personal experiences motivate you to explore a new version of yourself?

- What do you recognize tends to get in the way of your creativity most?

- What commitment are you willing to make to yourself to show respect, compassion, and acceptance to yourself?

- What do you want?

Reflective Pause:

To be honest, I am a bit emotional as I begin the final chapter of this book. I felt such a tugging on my heart for years. I longed to get down on paper a culmination of my personal experiences and share what I have learned up to this point. I do believe that the words that I have written do this duty justice. I can only hope that my words resonate with you on some level. If one plug for an idea comes to you as a reflection of something that you have read, that would fulfill my desires for this book. I am so proud of myself for sticking with the process. I have also recognized that there are many places in this book where I highlight my tendency to give up on projects or commitments. My life has proven that there have also been times where I never gave up, and I followed through with my mission. I am starting to recognize that I may have a cognitive distortion when it comes to my expectation that every goal will be met and recognized. I do not believe that anymore. Rather, I believe that we dedicate time, energy, and inspiration to what we feel called the most. Sometimes this comes with recognizing that past commitments are in fact getting in the way of our truest callings. This can be difficult to grapple with, and I urge you to seek out wise counsel through prayer to help you discern where your energy and love could be optimally utilized. For some, they choose to refrain from work to take care of their babies during their early years. For others, maybe it is a constant pruning of distractions that has helped to keep them grinding day in and out. Maybe an example of this would be limiting Netflix or social media. You get the gist of my thought process. I can promise that this journey was worth every leg of work. In just over two months, I fulfilled a life-long calling, and that is invaluable. Whatever your dream, I hope that my journey encourages you to start reaching. Start to filter the beliefs that tell you otherwise, and just start to Simply Begin . . .

Chapter 10: The Finale

"The last time always seems sad, but it isn't really. The end of one thing is only the beginning of another."

Laura Ingalls Wilder

Transitions and change are constant. When we resist change, we can often find ourselves in complex situations that can seem like we are on a never-ending hamster wheel of despair. The truth is that growth and change will always occur. We cannot force our babies to stay newborns, or magically find ourselves back in the glory days of our college years. We cannot bring back loved ones or cherished moments. Regret can be a constant experience if we are lost in the rat race of life. How many times have you looked back on a certain season of life and thought, "Gosh, I wish I would have realized how simple or sweet life was then?" My argument is that regret can often come from the recognition of our lack of presence. If we are so busy planning, worrying, or stressed about problems outside of our realm of control, we will miss the magic of the moment just the way that it is now. These philosophies are what have resulted from my own experience evolving from living for the future vs. living now. This book is a result of a simple decision. I have always wanted to become an author. I feel inspired by my life experience and education, and I had to find a way to express myself in a way that feels authentic and true to my current season. I do not like to think in black and white. In fact, this concept is referred to as "cognitive distortion" in my line of work. I also believe this concept pertains to what I am trying to convey. If you want to move towards change in your life, you can begin now. This journey has hopefully paved the way for you to explore yourself in a thoughtful, intentional way. I often meet with clients who feel as if they have lost themselves, and I want to challenge you to believe that your heart is always available to you. We will face challenges, relationships, losses, and disappointments. These moments test our resiliency and force us to grow in ways we cannot fully anticipate. Through these moments, we often choose to keep our spirits guarded and hidden. In one sense, it is appropriate to take time and space to process the transitions, and this stage is not meant to continue indefinitely.

Proverbs 4:25-26 states:

> "Let your eyes look straight ahead; fix your gaze directly before you. Give careful thought to the paths for your feet and be steadfast in all your ways."

One beautiful truth to life is the fact that we are always presented with paths to choose. We can continue to loop around and take paths we are familiar with, and lead to disappointing destinations. We can also choose to change directions. This can be an intimidating choice due to the uncertain journey that lies ahead, and I am here to tell you that life will continue to present you with options. Logic and protection will heir towards safety and familiarity, which is a beautiful truth that we can thank our autonomic nervous system for providing for us. Creativity, passion, and purpose may ask us to step into the unknown. Only you can discern what your next step may be, and only you can speak to God regarding the unique calling He has instilled into your heart.

We are not marked by what we go through, but we are presented with the opportunity to choose how to respond or change. Our God wants us to have *life* in the fullest possible way. I certainly cannot imagine that He designed you for endless workdays and feeling obsessively connected to your phone and the internet. That just cannot be "it". That cannot be life.

We are meant to *live freely*. So, take the chance. Start to daydream. You have the time, power, and ability to use your most valuable tool, your story and rewrite your future.

Bibliography

Angelou, Maya. *Rainbow in the Cloud: The Wisdom and Spirit of Maya Angelou*. New York, NY: Caged Bird Legacy & Penguin Random House, 2014.

NYU Drama Therapy As Performance Series, I Don't Wanna Go There excerpt from: *Behind the Doors: Terror in the Home and in the World*. New York City, November 10-13, 2016.

Rumi. *Rumi: The Beloved Is You*, Your Body is a Guest House. Translated by Shahram Shiva. Poem used by permission of the Rumi network, 2021.

Recommended Reading:

Linehan, M. M. *DBT? Skills Training Handouts and Worksheets, Second Edition*. Guilford, 2014.

Pederson, L. *The Expanded Dialectical Behavior Therapy Skills Training Manual, 2nd Edition: Dbt for Self-Help and Individual & Group Treatment Settings*. PESI, 2017.

Van Dijk, S. *Calming the emotional storm: Using Dialectical Behavior Therapy Skills to Manage Your Emotions and Balance Your Life*. New Harbinger, 2012.

www.ingramcontent.com/pod-product-compliance
Lightning Source LLC
Chambersburg PA
CBHW070737030726
47601CB00001B/51